THIS BOOK IS
A GIFT FROM:

_____

TO:

_____

BECAUSE:

_____

_____

TRANSFORMING
ORDINARY PEOPLE
INTO...

FUNDRAISING
SUPERHEROES!

...EVEN THOSE WHO HATE TO ASK

BY CAROL WEISMAN, MSW, CSP

WHAT NONPROFIT LEADERS HAVE TO SAY...

Any reader will never think about fundraising as a chore, again! In tight times such as these, this isn't a book, it's a life preserver!

BETTY STALLINGS

Highly accessible. Brief but real. Well suited for board members with busy lives and want to get to the point.

REV. JERRY PAUL
President and CEO
Deaconess Foundation

Just read Carol's new book and my sides hurt from laughing. And the best part is that the enjoyment came while learning many really, truly useful tips on how to fundraise, especially if you think you can't..

SUSAN J. ELLIS, President, Energize, Inc., consultant in volunteerism and often a money-hunting board member

As a long-time board member, I didn't realize how much I had to offer as a fundraiser. I can't wait to implement some of these great ideas.

MARGO GREEN, JD
Green Cordonnier & House LLP
Board Member, Kids in the Middle

A "spoonful of sugar" helps make the dose of an otherwise dry subject of fundraising more appealing and enjoyable to read. I simply loved everything in this book and then asked my wife to read it and she too enjoyed it.

SANDY PETERS, Director of Development
Animal Protective Association of Missouri

Superheroes truly succeeds in taking the "wince factor" out of fundraising for everyone. This is another how-to winner for Carol and nonprofits everywhere!

ALAN BROWNSTEIN, Executive Director Ntl. Alliance for Thrombosis and Thrombophilia

I enjoyed this book and learned new information. (I guess after being the United Jewish Appeal National Campaign Training Director and producing programs to train people to fund raise I would have heard it all!)

ANITA JACOBS, PhD, CSP

Down to earth advice for a tough subject for non-profits, laced—not drenched—with humor to help us understand it is not rocket science. Practical tips and techniques applicable to any nonprofit organi-zation, coupled with memorable vignettes that allow the reader to actually remember the advice.

GLENN PIERCE, MD, PhD.

In *Fundraising Superheroes* Carol shows how easy it can be with her witty ideas and clever illus-tra-tions. This book will be a shot of confidence and a game plan for nonprofit organizations every-where! Afterall, it's not brain surgery!

ALLISON COLLINGER, AHC Consulting LLC

WHAT NONPROFIT LEADERS HAVE TO SAY...

This awesome! I learned a ton just from reading these few pages. I love the humor, the accessibility, Everything. We will use it as our New Testament!

JEFFREY ROSE, MD Co-Founder African Health and Hospital Foundation

Carol's quirky, brilliant style comes through on every page. The information is tactical, practical and proven—she backs up just about every point with a clear example so that there is absolutely no excuse for the reader not to "get it." A great, user-friendly guidebook for caring people who want to super-size their fundraising success.

GAIL S. MELTZER, CFRE
CoreStrategies for Nonprofits, Inc.

In typical Carol style *Fundraising Superheroes* is a no-nonsense approach with a step-by-step outline for board member fundraising with just a touch of humor. It addresses the needs of a large well estab-lished group as well as the fledging organization. With specific hands-on examples this book can jumpstart the fundraising efforts of any group. I recommend this book to all my fundraising "heroes"!!

ZOE WOOD LYLE, Executive Director
Bar Association of Metropolitan St. Louis
and the St. Louis Bar Foundation

Terrific! Carol has again created an authoritative work that is both comprehensive and non-threat-ening—written under the guise of humor and plain talk. This is an easy-to-read guide that you will refer to again-and-again when approaching any fund-raising or relationship-building challenge.

DICK HELLNER
Past President, Prevent Blindness America

WHAT NONPROFIT LEADERS HAVE TO SAY...

I'm a Carol Weisman groupie! Who else could make the subject of fundraising entertaining? This book is fun and a fast read and her examples to get the point across are right on target. Read this book and you will be a CW groupie, too.

TERRY JO GILE, the Safety Lady ®
Past-President, Clinical Laboratory Management Assoc., St. Louis Chapter, and Ntl. Board Member

Carol once again relates her real and at times humorous life experiences and stories to the world of fundraising.

BRENT A. TAYLOR, Director of Planned Giving & Endowment Development
United Way of Greater Chattanooga

After my love affair with *The Incredibles*, I thought I would never fall in love again. I was wrong. My heart embraced Carol's *Fundraising Superheroes* even more! The practical strategies, tips, cartoons, traps to avoid and hints were a boon. The stories of ordinary people doing extraordinary things were inspiring...and laughter was in no short supply. An absolute MUST READ for a board raising the bar from orientation to the finishing line.

TESSE AKPEKI,
OnBoard consultant, London, England

Well you did it again! You have a way of writing that makes it easy for everyone to understand. I am ordering copies for each of our board members and additional copies to distribute to boards of children charities we work with. Congratulations!

NORM MOENCKHAUS
Executive Director,
YouthBridge Community Foundation

TRANSFORMING ORDINARY PEOPLE INTO...
FUNDRAISING SUPERHEROES
...EVEN THOSE WHO HATE TO ASK

F.E. Robbins & Sons Press

Cover design by: R-H Design Group and EFG Publishing, Inc.

Cartoons by: Dennis Fletcher

Cover, Author & Dedication Photography by: Suzy Gorman

Page Design by: Elaine Floyd, EFG Publishing, Inc.

Printed by: RR Donnelley & Sons

ISBN-13: 978-0-9789678-1-9

13 12 11 10 09   5 4 3 2 1

Printed in the United States of America

To order additional copies of this title, contact 314-863-4422 or

WWW.FUNDRAISINGSUPERHEROES.COM

DEDICATION...

FOR MY GRANDSON,
FRANK EDWARD ROBBINS VI,
AKA FREDDY,
OUR
"SUPER GRANDSON"

PICTURED ABOVE: JONATHAN ROBBINS
AKA JONO, LAURA ROBBINS, FRANK EDWARD
ROBBINS VI, AKA FREDDY, FRANK EDWARD
ROBBINS V, AKA TEDDY, CAROL WEISMAN,
AKA OMA, FRANK EDWARD ROBBINS IV, AKA OPA.

(WITH ALL THE ALIASES YOU'D THINK THE WHOLE
FAMILY IS IN SHOW BIZ OR THE WITNESS
PROTECTION PROGRAM!)

CONTENTS

HOW TO READ THIS BOOK

Fundraising is a team sport. Everyone on your board and fundraising team needs to take a look at your copy or, better still, have their own. Mark it up, or if writing in books pains your reader's soul, use stickers to mark your favorite ideas and, as a group, decide what makes sense for your team.

I think fundraising is also like baking. When I was in college, I tried to bake one of my mother's German chocolate cakes that was delightful in St. Louis, but turned out the consistency of a hockey puck in mile-high Denver. What makes sense for a small local nonprofit might fall flat for a national with multiple chapters, or vice-versa. You need to measure talent and risk and the atmosphere of both your board and your donors and decide what is in sync with your mission and your needs.

JIM LIED TO ME...

He wasn't the first man to do it. I had just started to work with a new client. The executive director, a brilliant attorney, told me that her board president Jim wasn't much of a fundraiser. Jim concurred.

I went to their annual gala. I asked a sleek young man how he came to come to this fete. He told me that his friend Jim asked him to purchase a ticket. Two more slender guys joined our group. They were also FOJ's (friends of Jim). It turns out Jim asked his whole marathon group to buy tickets. There was an entire posse of guys who looked liked beef jerky and women who wore a size 2 toddler who were FOJ's. He brought 17 people, many of whom became donors or volunteers to an event. To me, that makes Jim a great fundraiser.

Both Jim and the E.D. thought he wasn't a fundraiser. I said to myself, "Self, you've gotta write a book to help board members realize that to be a truly great fundraiser, you can do any number of things."

Because I speak and train on fundraising all over the world, I have tried to "steal" from the best.

If you have a better idea or a way to improve what is in the next edition, let me know.

Get ready to don your cape (tights optional)!

--CAROL

FICTION AND FACT...

#1 EVERYONE KNOWS THAT IF PEOPLE JOIN A BOARD, THEY ARE EXPECTED TO FUNDRAISE. In fact, no one joins a nonprofit board because it is a great opportunity to fundraise and many are clueless that they are supposed to. You might have joined for any number of reasons: Perhaps you've been personally affected by the cause such as cancer or drug abuse, or you want to maintain something that is meaningful to you like the symphony or the environment or sometimes its just because the right person asks. The reasons are as unique and varied as the people who serve. The bottom line is that if you accept this great honor, and it is a great honor to serve on a board, fundraising is one of your responsibilities.

#2 YOU HAVE TO ASK FOR MONEY to be a good fundraiser. The truth is, you can be a great fundraiser without ever asking for money. That is what this book is all about. Fundraising is a process and you can get involved anywhere in the process and make an incredible difference to your organization. You do NOT have to make the ask.

#3 TIME IS MONEY. Time is not money. You might be thinking, "Oh, I give my time, why should I have to write a check as well?" It is like going to the doctor and saying, "I had an x-ray, why do I need a blood test?" Both are important, but they aren't the same thing. Your time is of great value. It will not, however, keep the lights on, pay the staff or the rent.

...IN FUNDRAISING

#4 UNRESTRICTED MONEY IS THE ONLY KIND OF MONEY TO REQUEST. Actually, all kinds of money are great. I recently worked with a group that only wanted to raise unrestricted money so that members could decide how to spend the donations to their group. The year before, they had raised $6000 with an end-of-the-year mail appeal. Earlier in the year, they raised $900,000 in restricted funds for a football field. One needs a certain amount of pragmatism. Many donors want to give restricted dollars. Make it work.

#5 WE CAN FORM A GROUP THAT WILL RAISE FUNDS and turn it over to us to spend. You might be thinking, why can't we just form a fundraising board or a leadership council to raise the money and the board will decide how to spend it? The truth is, rich people don't raise money and give it to poor people to spend. This is true whether they earned, married or inherited their money. They stay wealthy by controlling it. There are exceptions, such as organizations that are highly homogeneous like Jewish Federations or Catholic Charities or the Italian American Society. Sal might raise the money one year and let his brother-in-law Max spend it and they reverse roles the next year. The reasons this works is that they share values and culture. The more diverse the organization, the less likely this is to happen. Therefore, it's the board's job.

FICTION AND FACT...

#6 I CAN'T SURVIVE ASKING SOMEONE FOR MONEY and being turned down. Friedrich Nietzsche wrote, "That which will not kill you shall make you strong." He was clearly referring to fundraising. The truth of the matter is that, to the best of my knowledge, no one ever died of fundraising. (Although the same cannot be said of having sex outside of marriage. But that is another book!) As my friend says, "Sometimes people say no, but they will never hit you."

#7 STAFF WILL RAISE THE MONEY. You may be thinking, "But we have staff. Why should I be doing the fundraising?" It is like a truffle hound and a farmer. You work in partnership. One sniffs it out and the other picks it up. The job of staff is to make the board effective and vice-versa.

#8 BUILD IT AND THEY WILL COME. The most common reason people don't give is that they aren't asked. If you have ever said, "We are the best kept secret in town," knock it off. Time to tell everyone what you do and what you need. On the other hand, if you rave about how wonderful your organization is, folks might assume that you don't need financial help. You need to make sure they know that they are invited to be a part of something wonderful and significant.

...IN FUNDRAISING

#9 WE HAVE A FUNDRAISING COMMITTEE, SO I DON'T HAVE TO DO IT. The work of the development or fundraising committee is not to do all of the work but to make sure it gets done. You might have experienced the frustration of making numerous calls to get something done and come away with the thought, "It is easier to do it myself." This might be true in the short run, but you won't build organizational capacity by adopting this approach.

#10 BOARD MEMBERS MUST BE INVOLVED IN EVERY ASPECT OF FUNDRAISING. All board members have their own kryptonite. Some board members will lose their superpowers at a special event or when asked to make an introduction or make an ask, while others will do anything but a spreadsheet, attend another meeting or pick up a phone. Ask your folks what they want to do and what they don't want to do. Respect their vulnerability, and ask if they are willing to do something with training and a partner or if they want to do something else. Then listen closely.

#11 WE ARE GOING TO RAISE MONEY LIKE OBAMA, small amounts from large numbers of donors. If you are in the media 24 hours a day month after month for several years, the Obama fundraising strategy will work. If you have a web site that has 1 or 2 million visitors, a web-based strategy makes sense. If you get more than 50% of your money from state funds, you need to see your legislators on a regular basis. You need a clear strategy and a solid plan that fits your board, your organization and your needs.

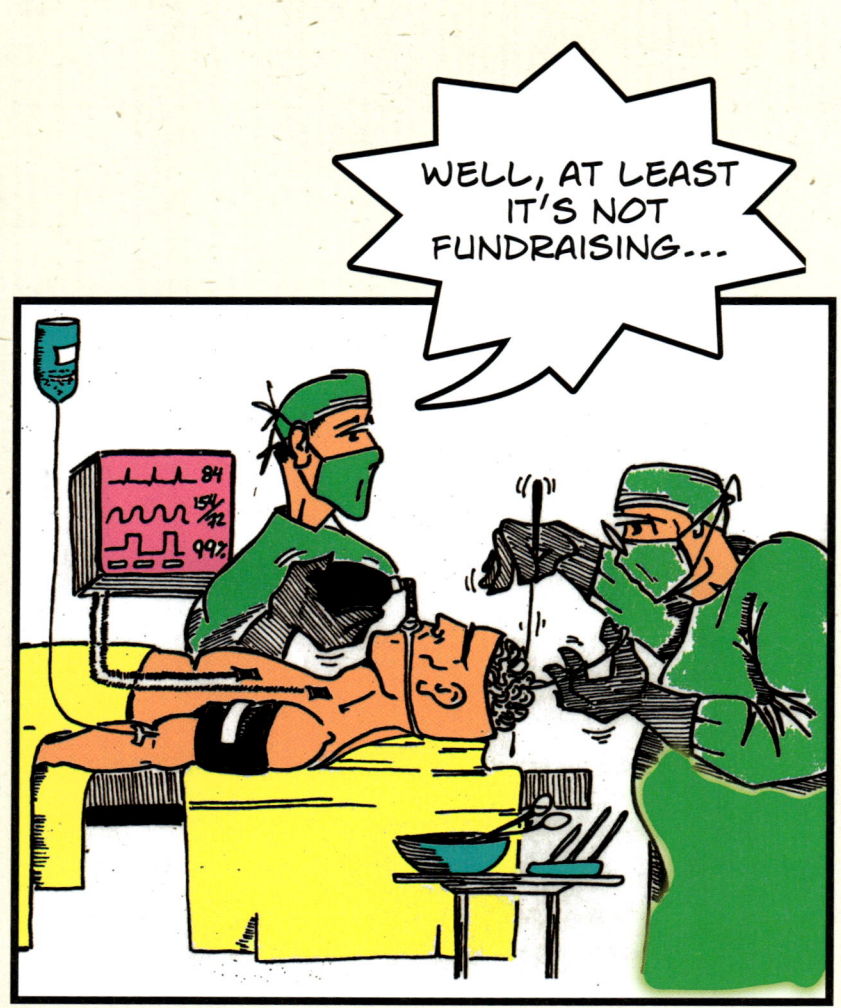

1

STARTING...

WITH YOU!

You can't sell what you don't know. You need to understand what your organization does, how it does it and what your role is before you take the first step.

The more important the job you have, the more training you get. If people's lives are in your hands, let's say you're a pilot or a doctor, you get a whole lot of training. If you are a board member, people's lives are also in your hands. It might not take 8 or 10 years, but 8 or 10 minutes would be nice. A few hours even better.

Board members are fiscally responsible for the organization. Put some skin in the game. You might write your check for a different amount than you would ask for, but you need to make your own commitment first.

Why do you have to give your money if you are also giving your time? Other donors expect it. If the people closest to the heart of the organization haven't supported this cause, why should anyone else? Foundations demand it and will often decline a grant request if they don't think the board is doing its part.

You might be wondering how much to give. It should be an amount you feel proud of. It might be a first installment of a pledge for a larger amount.

Make a donation before you do anything else. 100% board giving is an absolute minimum.

If you haven't made your own donation, put this book down, go to your computer, checkbook or wallet and make it happen. NOW!

READ YOUR MISSION STATEMENT

What does your organization say it does? You don't need to memorize the mission statement. You simply need to be able to tell people in your own way what your organization does.

Mission statements come in all sizes and shapes, just like board members. They outline what your nonprofit is supposed to do. They are also legal documents and on file with the secretary of state, which is why they are sometimes less than Pulitzer Prize-worthy.

PUT THE MISSION STATEMENT IN YOUR OWN WORDS

This is sometimes called "an elevator speech." Some mission statements roll off the tongue. Some mission statements are quite formal due to tradition, legal requirement or national-chapter dictates. Find a way to quickly describe what your organization does that is intriguing and invites questions. Breathe life into your mission statement. Use personal anecdotes to show how your organization has actually helped an individual, a family or a community.

Then test it out on other board members and friends. Make sure everyone on your board is on the same elevator.

EXAMPLE: I was working in Washington DC for Rebuilding Together. I literally stepped on the elevator with a group of Rebuilding Board members and Mary Kay reps, who were attending a conference in the same hotel. One of the sweet-smelling Mary Kay gals asked, "What is Rebuilding Together?" A woman from Alaska said, "We rehab houses for the poor and elderly. Where I live in Alaska, we primarily work on roofs." She then added, "You all must sell Mary Kay. I recognize the cologne, the pink outfits and love your products. Would you like some info about Rebuilding Together?" When we hit the ground floor, we stepped out and exchanged business cards. Not bad for 6 floors of travel.

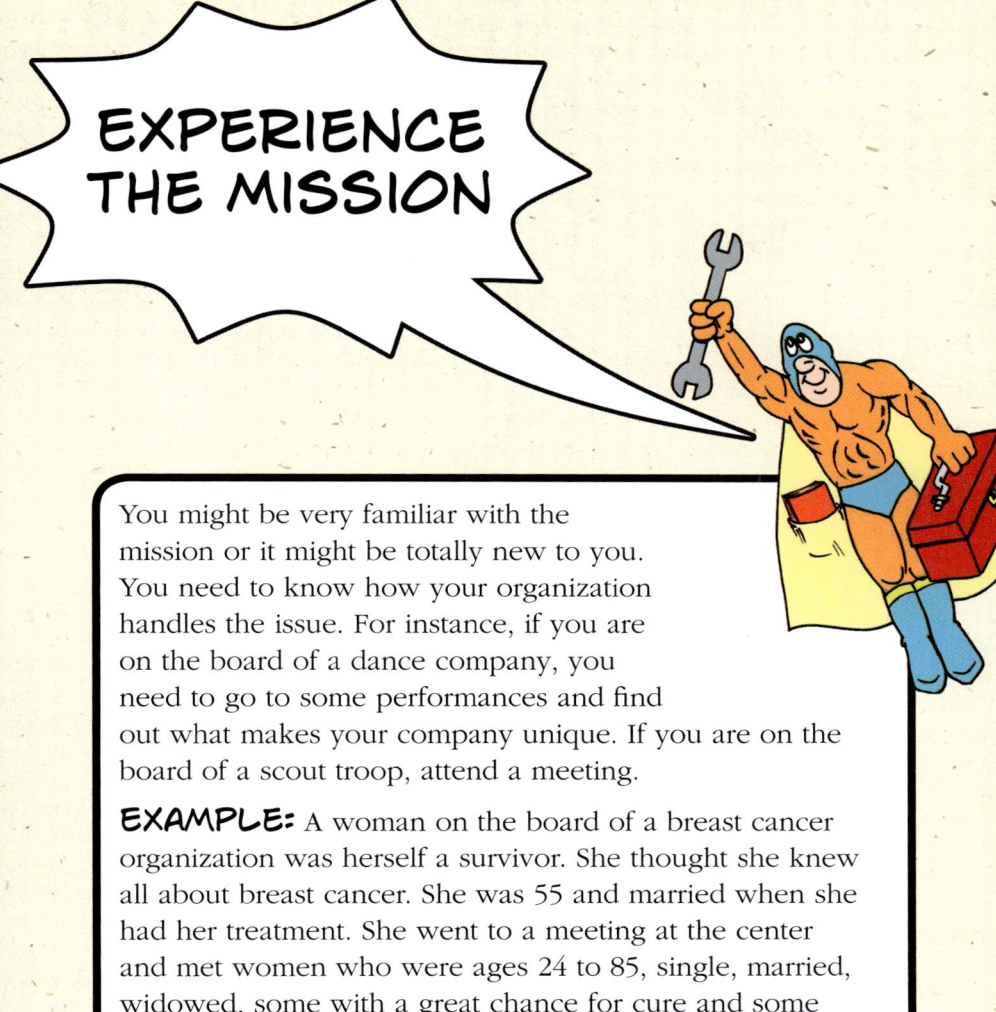

EXPERIENCE THE MISSION

You might be very familiar with the mission or it might be totally new to you. You need to know how your organization handles the issue. For instance, if you are on the board of a dance company, you need to go to some performances and find out what makes your company unique. If you are on the board of a scout troop, attend a meeting.

EXAMPLE: A woman on the board of a breast cancer organization was herself a survivor. She thought she knew all about breast cancer. She was 55 and married when she had her treatment. She went to a meeting at the center and met women who were ages 24 to 85, single, married, widowed, some with a great chance for cure and some with little hope for optimism. She said, "I thought my experience was the norm. I'm so glad I went to a meeting. I understand what we do and how we do it. I now see that my experience is just that—my experience."

GIVE A CHALLENGE GIFT

People love a challenge. And you can leverage your gift into an even greater amount. Be creative. If you want younger donors, match the gifts of anyone under 30 two to one. If you want the staff to give, match their gifts. Consider a multi-generational challenge. If your current donors are older, ask grandparents to ask their children and grandchildren to give. Put a cap on your giving as well as a time limit.

ASK YOUR EMPLOYER ABOUT BOARD SERVICE

If you are working full time and not self-employed, discuss your plans to join a board with your employer. You might need time off occasionally or on a regular basis for board activities, or there might be a conflict of interest, a moral or legal issue. (This sometimes comes up when you want time off from your job at a privately-owned company with different values than the political action committee you want to spend time on.)

Some employers have funds or foundations that match your gifts. When you are supported by your employer, you might not only get time but also money for your nonprofit and recognition for your community leadership. Plus, your employer's directors and officers' insurance might extend to your nonprofit service.

Some companies allow their employees to use company resources including office supplies, telephones, photocopiers, and clerical support for routine tasks. They may be willing to pay for your travel time and expenses to attend board and committee meetings. Others will insist that you do all your board and committee work on your own time and at your own expense at home. It's important to have this discussion up front with your employer before you make a commitment to the nonprofit organization that invited you to serve on their board.

Whether you know about the mission "up close and personal" or got involved because of a friend or employer, write out your journey with the mission. Share your feelings and thoughts, what shocked, delighted, appalled, or pleased you as you got involved. It might be the story of how your father was diagnosed with Alzheimer's and his subsequent death, or your first home visit with a nurse to visit a newborn or your experience as a Special Olympics coach. Don't worry about verbs, paragraphs, or spelling. Get it on paper.

Then share it with your board as a "mission moment" to begin a meeting or as part of a board retreat. Ask each board member to do this. You will have a treasure trove of quotable material for use in printed materials, newsletters, websites and the like.

Invite people. DO NOT make it mandatory.

EXAMPLE: Many years ago I chaired a board of an organization whose mission was to end the cycle of child abuse. A facilitator asked everyone to do just such an exercise. One woman abruptly left the room in tears. She later shared with me that she was on the board because she had been an abuser, sought treatment, and dreaded another mother having no other parenting skills besides the ability to strike a child. This is governance, not therapy, and boundaries have to be respected.

UNDERSTAND HOW THE SECTOR WORKS AND WHERE THE MONEY COMES FROM

TAKE THIS QUIZ:

According to Giving USA, in 2007

Of the 306.39 billion in contributions:

Corporations gave ___%

Individuals gave ___%

Foundations gave ___%

Bequests resulted in ___%

If you came within 5 points on each category, reward yourself with a $100,000 Grand bar. You understand money. Just for taking the quiz, you get a PowerBar.

Corporations: 5.1% ($15.69 Billion), Individuals, 74.8% ($229.03 Billion), Foundations, 12.6% ($38.52 Billion), Bequests, 7.6% ($23.15 Billion)

> ## WRITE YOUR NONPROFIT INTO YOUR WILL

CAROL AND FRANK

I have my favorite nonprofits in my will for three reasons:

1. I don't plan to die.

2. I don't miss the money today.

3. I don't want my husband's next wife to get my money!!!

Approximately 60% of all Americans don't have a will. Just having one puts you ahead of the curve, and when you include your values in your will, you communicate them to your kids.

FRANK'S NEW WIFE WHO WILL NOT GET CAROL'S MONEY BECAUSE IT IS GOING TO CHARITY

MAKE SURE
THERE IS
A SYSTEM
TO TRACK GIFTS

If you are a new organization, you MUST have a system to track your gifts. There are many great integrated software packages out there. You can get from point A to point B on a bicycle or in a Rolls Royce.

It you are a mature organization, ask staff if they have the tools they need to work efficiently. If you don't, consider donating the funds to upgrade.

RESOURCES: Go to your nearest Association of Fundraising Professionals Chapter (www.AFPnet.org) and ask for their recommendations. Also, check out www.nten.org, Nonprofit Technology Network, for their recommendations.

FOR YOUR NEXT SPECIAL OCCASION, ASK FOR A GIFT TO YOUR NONPROFIT

Many of us have enough "stuff." (And some of us have relatives and friends with hideous taste.) When you are getting married for the 6th or 7th time or hitting the big 40, 50 or 60, ask your posse to give a gift to your nonprofit rather than fill your crib with stuff you don't need.

EXAMPLE: When the family of a Holocaust survivor wanted to give him an 85th birthday party, he requested "no presents." So, in his honor, his children, grandchildren and great-grandchildren made a donation of both time and family memorabilia to a Holocaust museum. At his party, the youngest great grandchild who was not an infant was one of the speakers. This five-year-old child said, "We will never forget." The survivor said it was the best birthday of his life.

REVIEW HOW MONEY IS SPENT

When you go in to make an ask, you are going to be asked financial information. You don't need to memorize the last financial statement, but you do need to know information like the gross income, the cost of a unit of service, salaries and overhead. You will want to review your 990, the federal tax return for nonprofits. You can look up tax information of your organization and other nonprofits at www.GuideStar.org.

CULTIVATING...

2

YOUR PROSPECTS

If fundraising were seeking a life partner, this would be the dating phase. Cultivation is all about seeing if there is a good fit.

EXAMPLE: If you are interested in domestic violence, there are any number of organizations that do this kind of work. Which one is the best fit for your philanthropic investment? Are you more interested in an agency that does education or provides therapy or offers job training? Are you interested in giving to a shelter that accepts older children and has a therapeutic day care? Do your want to support a shelter that espouses your religious beliefs? It takes time and effort for the donor to make the right choice.

Cultivation is the process by which the nonprofit shouts, shares or blares "pick me."

INVITE A POTENTIAL DONOR TO A SPECIAL EVENT

Fill your table with potential donors.

It should be like the perfect blind date between possible contributor and charity. A gentle, non-threatening introduction can take place at a special event. It might be love at first sight or your guest might show only a slight interest.

The evening should be followed by a call that starts with, "What did you think of our organization? And ultimately, "Would you like to learn more?"

RESEARCH A POTENTIAL DONOR

Use the web to find out what your potential donor has given to in the past. A simple Google search is a great place to begin. You might want to check out www.NOZAsearch.com as another source of donor information.

Social networking tools such as Facebook, MySpace and LinkedIn are great to find out if you have friends and interests in common.

ARE YOU SURE THERE ISN'T AN EASIER WAY TO DO DONOR RESEARCH?

RESEARCH A FOUNDATION

Many large foundations generally fund as few as 2 out of 100 applications. One of the primary reasons for this is that you might be asking them to fund something that is not their focus. For instance, the foundation might only fund children's issues and you are a geriatric center. Don't waste your time or theirs.

EXAMPLE: An astute board member researched a foundation before she went in to make the ask. At the meeting, the first thing she did was quote the mission of the foundation and then explained why her nonprofit and the foundation were such a perfect fit. The foundation director said that in 11 years of making grants no one had ever quoted the foundation's mission. He was not only bowled over by the diligence of the board member, he agreed with her case for giving and funded the request.

RESEARCH A CORPORATION

They are many ways into a corporation. The best is to have a personal link to the economic decision makers. You can get in through the marketing department, the community relations department or the foundation. Discover which is the best fit. Sometimes, you will do better to ask for something other than money.

EXAMPLE: A volunteer went to a friend who was the CEO of a medium-sized corporation and asked for a donation of $1000, an average gift for this company. The CEO said that they were laying off staff and not giving any more gifts this year. The volunteer then asked if she could have 10 hours of the public relations department's time. Not only did she get the time, the P.R. department asked their vendors to support the cause and over 150 employees came out for the nonprofit's walk.

BRING A GROUP TO YOUR CHARITY'S VENUE FOR A MEETING

Ask your religious group, women's or men's club to visit your nonprofit for their next meeting so that they can learn where it is and what it does.

EXAMPLE: A new geriatric facility made its community room available for nonprofits to have their meetings and offered tours. In the first year, approximately 12 of their residents came from referrals from people who had come to meetings.

BRING FRIENDS, RELATIVES AND COLLEAGUES TO YOUR NONPROFIT FOR A TOUR

When "touring for dollars" make sure you ask your guests what they already know about your cause and give lots of opportunities to ask questions about how they can get involved. A good tour should have at least 50% of the talking done by the guests.

If your organization has a development professional on staff, take a few minutes to call him or her after the tour and share your impressions. Your guests may have shared information about their past history with the organization, about their motivations for involvement with the group, or about their interest in becoming more active in the nonprofit's activities. When appropriate, have a follow-up plan such as a one-on-one meeting about giving opportunities with the development director or other employee, such as a physician, professor, or other service provider.

HAVE AN "AT HOME" FOR YOUR FRIENDS AND RELATIVES

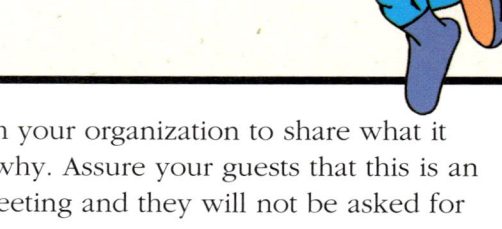

Invite a rep from your organization to share what it does, how and why. Assure your guests that this is an informational meeting and they will not be asked for money.

EXAMPLE: An alternative school for high school students in Massachusetts had an "at home" hosted by one of the graduate's grandparents. Friends of current parents were invited. Five graduates shared how this school transformed their lives. Despite the fact that the guests were not asked to give, the school raised $35,000.

GO ON THE SPEAKING CIRCUIT ABOUT YOUR CAUSE

Many organizations such as Rotary, the Junior League, etc. have weekly or monthly speakers. These are great organizations that are full of potential donors and volunteers.

Create a "stump speech" that includes a poignant case, how your audience can get involved and a clear call to action. If you are new to speaking, join Toastmasters, www.Toastmasters.org. If you are an experienced speaker, consider looking into The National Speaker's Organization, www.NSASpeaker.org.

EDWARD LEIGH, MA, COLORECTAL CANCER SURVIVOR, SPEAKS ABOUT HIS EXPERIENCES EVERYWHERE FROM "THE TODAY SHOW" TO HOSPITAL STAFFS WORLDWIDE.

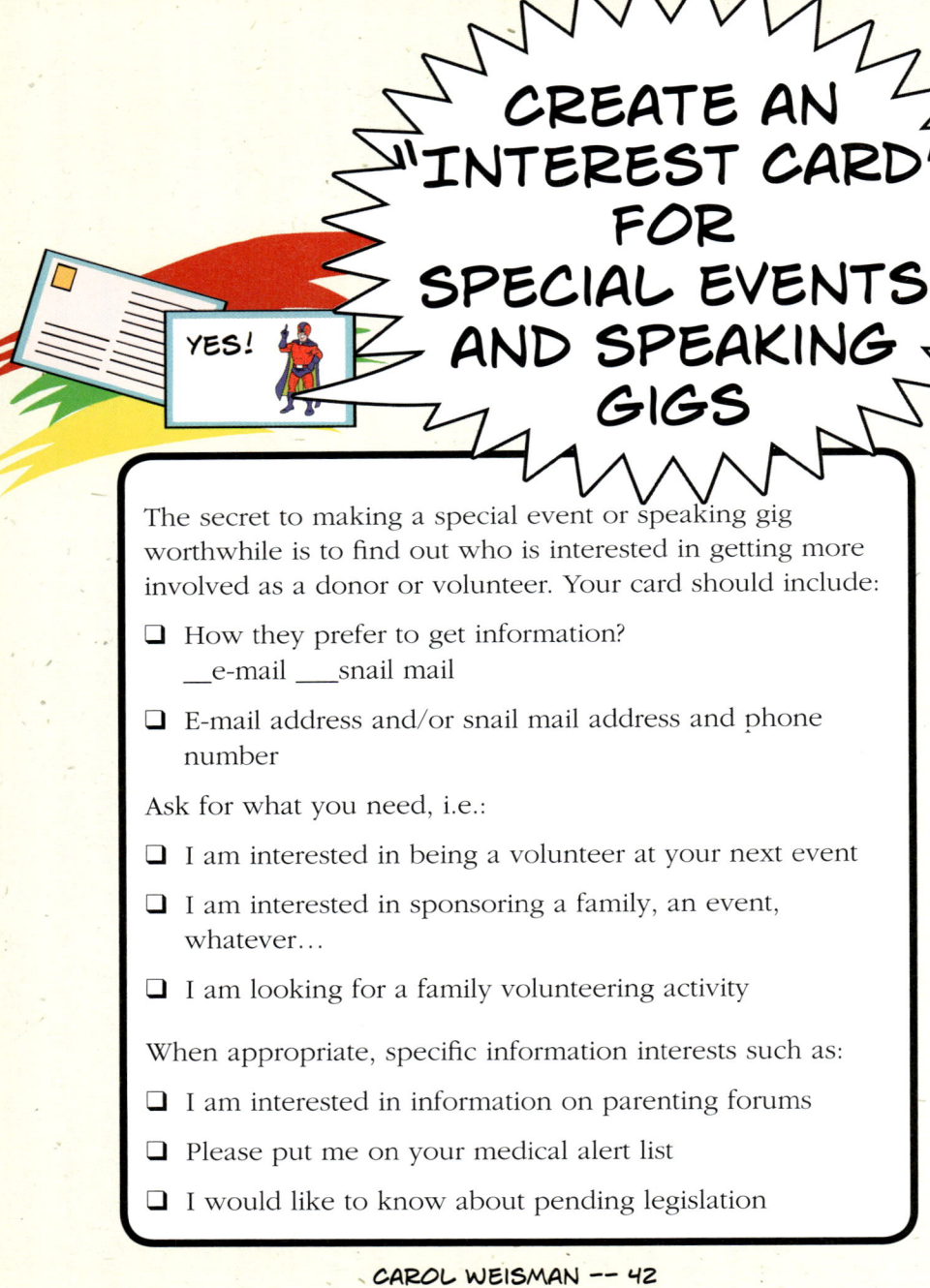

CREATE AN "INTEREST CARD" FOR SPECIAL EVENTS AND SPEAKING GIGS

YES!

The secret to making a special event or speaking gig worthwhile is to find out who is interested in getting more involved as a donor or volunteer. Your card should include:

❑ How they prefer to get information?
  __e-mail ___snail mail

❑ E-mail address and/or snail mail address and phone number

Ask for what you need, i.e.:

❑ I am interested in being a volunteer at your next event

❑ I am interested in sponsoring a family, an event, whatever…

❑ I am looking for a family volunteering activity

When appropriate, specific information interests such as:

❑ I am interested in information on parenting forums

❑ Please put me on your medical alert list

❑ I would like to know about pending legislation

SHARE YOUR E-MAIL AND "SNAIL MAIL" LISTS

A clear list that has accurate phone, e-mail and address is invaluable in soliciting funds. It is helpful to share any relevant information such as your friends' workplaces (perhaps with matching programs) and family foundations.

The more controversial your cause, the more important this is. The most polarizing cause is abortion; probably the least is cancer care for children. A history, strong feelings or personal experiences are extremely helpful when making a face-to-face request.

This, too, must be done cautiously. Before an organization shares its lists, it must have in place an "opt-in" or "opt-out" policy that allows its members and donors to indicate whether or not their names may be shared with like-minded organizations. It needs to be publicized via newsletters, annual giving pledge cards, membership forms and the like.

HAVE A MOVIE NIGHT THAT EXPLAINS YOUR MISSION

There are great films exploring any number of issues, from homelessness, alcoholism, abuse, and racism to dance, music and teaching.

Have a movie night in your home or a larger venue and have experts from your organization talk about how you are addressing these problems. Or you might want to partner with a local college or university and use their staff to lead a panel discussion.

Here are a few ideas to start the creative juices flowing:

Developmental Disabilities—Riding the Bus with My Sister

Genocide—Hotel Rwanda

Racism—Crash, Gran Torino

Homelessness—The Pursuit of Happyness, The Soloist

Alcoholism—When A Man Loves A Woman, 28 Days, Clean and Sober

Education—Stand and Deliver, Freedom Writers, The Class

Music—Mr. Holland's Opus, Music of the Heart

Dance—Billy Elliot, Center Stage

Make sure there is plenty of time for discussion. Popcorn is a must!

SHARE GROUP MAILING LISTS WITH YOUR NONPROFIT

If you belong to a sorority, fraternity, professional or service organization, share the mailing list with your nonprofit. Obviously, make sure you aren't violating the by-laws of the other organization.

EXAMPLE: With permission, a Junior League member announced to the entire membership a giving opportunity in one of the League's focus areas for the year. Both dollars and volunteers flocked to a "done-in-a-day" event.

SET UP A MEETING WITH ONE OF YOUR CLIENTS... YOU DON'T HAVE TO ATTEND

Many folks whether realtors, decorators, physicians, lawyers or manicurists, can't easily ask clients for money. You might feel more comfortable setting up a meeting and then getting out of the way. It can go something like this, "I know you are interested in X and I'm on a board that deals with this issue. I am wondering if you would like to meet the board president or executive director?"

You might want to keep literature about your organization or staff business cards in your waiting room or desk.

EXAMPLE: The Epilepsy Foundation of Northern California has memo pads, something like prescription pads, so that doctors can refer their patients for services or so that patients can become volunteers. This places the initiative on the patient and respects the patient and family confidentiality.

VISIT A LEGISLATOR AND SHARE WHAT YOUR ORGANIZATION DOES FOR YOUR COMMUNITY

Legislators need to know what their constituents are concerned about. Making a cultivation call to inform a legislator about an issue is the first step in getting renewed or attracting additional or first-time funding. When your legislator is back in your district, invite him or her for a tour. Always mention that it will be a photo op and have a camera ready.

If you are not sure who your legislator is, The League of Women's Voters website is a great resource, www.LWV.org.

GREAT SOLICITORS FOCUS ON THEIR DONORS FIRST, NOT THEIR CAUSE.

MAKING...

3

THE ASK

Some people love to ask for money. For most, it is difficult at best. The biggest fear is being told "no."

A friend of mine who had been a battered child grew up to be a brilliant fundraiser. She always told me when I was anxious before an ask, "They may say no, but they never hit."

The major difference between sales in the corporate world and asking for funds in the non-profit world is that corporations train their folks and nonprofits rarely provide training, particularly to their board members. The solicitor has to be passionate, educated about the donor and the organization and have already made a gift. When you send the right person and ask for the right amount, you provide a wonderful opportunity for your donor to do good.

BEFORE YOU GO ON AN ASK, KNOW HOW MUCH YOU ARE GOING TO REQUEST

This takes research. It can be done using a web-based tool such as Wealth Engine, or the old fashioned way, by getting a group together who knows the community members, their wealth, and their giving history.

Always ask for a stretch gift.

EXAMPLE: On my 50th birthday, I was taken out for breakfast and asked for a gift of $10,000. When I stopped laughing, I explained that we had two kids in college. I also explained what I would be able to give. I suggested that my solicitors call at the end of the year (my birthday is January 19, in case you are interested!). Around March, I was making some changes in my will and put this organization in for $10,000. The amount was "sticky," meaning that it made sense and was reasonable. They didn't call at the end of the year, though. Follow-up is everything.

ASK FOR A MULTI-YEAR PLEDGE

Instead of asking for $50 or $1000, ask for that amount for 3 years. Think twice about asking for a longer period. What some organizations are finding about 5-year pledges is that the last two years are difficult to collect because of:

1. Changes in marital status

2. Changes in employment

3. Changes in staff at the nonprofit

4. Donor death

5. Donor moves out-of-town

6. Donor's diminished financial position

AGENDA

BE CLEAR WITH YOUR POTENTIAL DONOR WHAT YOU WANT TO DISCUSS

A friend of mine was called by an old boyfriend and asked out to lunch at a tony restaurant. She was very excited to reconnect. A new outfit and a French manicure later, she arrived to find out that he wanted to connect to her pocketbook, not her heart. Had he said, "I'm on the board of XYZ and want to discuss it with you," she would have been a lot more inclined to give.

DON'T AMBUSH PROSPECTS

WHEN WORKING WITH ANOTHER PERSON, MEET AT LEAST 15 MINUTES BEFORE GREETING YOUR PROSPECT

You want to get the chit chat out of the way before you go into a meeting. Before you get in the room, discuss everything from your child's soccer game to where you were able to park. That way, in the meeting, you can focus on the prospect. You also need to have a clear understanding about who is going to do what in the meeting and review any research on your donor.

COORDINATE WITH A PARTNER BEFORE MAKING AN ASK

Two people working together to make an ask can be a powerful force. You should have complementary rather than similar personalities and knowledge. For instance, one person can tell about the mission and money, another ask for the gift. A board-staff partnership works well.

When one member of the team is talking, his or her partner should be observing the prospect closely to watch for cues, such as body language and expressions of interest or concern, as well as to note the prospect's verbal responses.

EXAMPLE: When working with a voluntary health organization on fundraising training, I noticed one team had a much higher success rate than any other. I asked the group to think about what made them different from the other teams. Finally, a board member said, "One of us is a mom of a child with this disease and the other is a man with this condition." Every other team had people who were alike: two white guys ages 45-46, two moms, two physicians. Like many of us, they broke into teams with people they were comfortable with rather than with folks who complemented them. Once they reorganized, the giving rate went through the roof.

REVIEW THE LIST OF FOLKS GETTING SOLICITATION LETTERS AND WRITE A PERSONAL P.S. TO THOSE YOU KNOW

A personal P.S. will make a huge difference in your gift rate. Try something like: "Dear Judy, Really appreciate your considering a gift, Sal," or "Larry, how about using some of the money you won from me at golf for a good cause?"

START A LEGACY SOCIETY

If you don't already have a designation for those who have put your charity in their wills, start one. It is a way to share your commitment to your cause and inspire others to give a lasting gift as well.

My favorite planned giving quote was heard at a Chuck Loring lecture. He can't remember where he first heard it, so apologies to the creator of "Planned giving is like football. When you kick off, we receive."

RECRUIT ATTORNEYS TO WRITE WILLS AT NO COST TO YOUR DONORS

60% of all Americans die without a will. There are a myriad of reasons. If you are a large institution, you might want to consider having a full-time estate planning attorney either on staff or on retainer.

If you are a small nonprofit, you might want to ask local attorneys to write simple wills pro bono or at reduced fees.

You might also find a donor to pay the attorney's fees.

EXAMPLE: After the sale of Anheuser Busch to InBev in St. Louis, a friend's mother was going to receive an 8-figure check. She was in her 80's and wanted to give a chunk of the money to a local nonprofit. She and her husband, who had worked at the brewery, had been buying stock since 1945. She was somewhat out of touch with current legal prices and said, "I'm not going to pay any attorney hundreds of dollars to write my will." Her daughter found a donor to pay the legal fees and the agency received an enormous gift during this lady's lifetime. It was a major win-win.

START A GIVING SOCIETY

A giving society is a group of givers that donate at a specific level. Sometimes there are tiered levels and sometimes just a minimum. The levels are often related to the mission, such as the directors circle, producer, etc. for a theater group. Gems are very popular as are alloys: diamond donors, platinum, ruby, gold. Religious groups use various levels of angels. Be creative.

EXAMPLE: One of the most successful giving groups is the United Way Tocqueville Society. These are donors who give an annual gift of $10,000 minimum. The Society has national name recognition and a clearly defined giving level. They give great recognition. This is a group folks want to be a part of.

AFTER A DONOR MEETING, WRITE IN-DEPTH NOTES

Whether you "close the gift" or not, make notes about the discussion. Include objections, information about family, such as names of children, activities and anything else your prospect mentions. You never know when the information will come in handy. Also, don't procrastinate. What you remember decreases exponentially by the day.

EXAMPLE: A Red Cross board member made a large ask and kept meticulous notes. He included the names of the donor's children. When there was a tragic car accident he thought it might be the donor's teenage son. He checked his notes, and sure enough, it was the donor's son who had died. The board member immediately wrote a condolence letter. It made such an impression on the donor that the board member remembered the name of his son that when it came time to honor his son's memory, he chose the Red Cross.

SOLICIT CHURCHES, SYNAGOGUES, MOSQUES, SORORITIES, FRATERNITIES AND SERVICE CLUBS FOR DONATIONS

If you are active in a group, sometimes all it takes is a simple proposal or coffee with a professional or volunteer leader. You might be surprised at the warmth and graciousness of the welcome you get.

ASK FOR AN ON-GOING PLEDGE ON A CREDIT OR DEBIT CARD

Some donors who are on a budget might not be able to give $50 today but would gladly give $10 a month for a year. You need to make it easy to give.

Arrange for electronic fund transfers to be made on a pre-arranged basis – monthly, quarterly or at year end, according to the donor's preferences.

EXAMPLE: An under-thirty Dad I know was lamenting his inability to make a $50 end-of-the-year donation to his favorite charity. I asked if he could give $10. He said that wouldn't be a problem. I asked, "What about $10 a month for the next year?" He was thrilled with the idea and called the nonprofit with his credit card number.

CALL A FRIEND, COLLEAGUE OR RELATIVE AND ASK FOR AN APPOINTMENT TO TALK ABOUT YOUR NONPROFIT

The most difficult aspect of major donor solicitation is getting the appointment. Write out notes before you make the call. This is a solicitation call, not an ambush. Ask who else, besides the person you are talking to, is involved in making philanthropic decisions. Invite that person to attend as well. It might be a spouse, child or financial advisor.

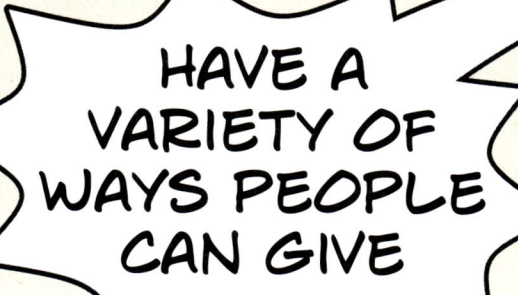

HAVE A VARIETY OF WAYS PEOPLE CAN GIVE

You might want to suggest a gift of stock, particularly if there has been a major stock transfer in your community (Anheuser Busch is a great example). You might request a gift over multiple years or months. You might suggest putting a gift on a credit card that you would process monthly or all at once. Some folks still like envelopes with stamps. The bottom line is that people want choice, not only in what they give to but also in how they give.

EXAMPLE: A development professional from "the big city" arrived in a small farming community in Iowa. She was having a heck of a time asking for monthly pledges when someone finally clued her in that farmers aren't paid monthly. They get a lump sum when the crop is sold. This small piece of information made a huge difference in her subsequent success rate.

FOLLOW UP WITH YOUR LONGTIME DONORS AND ASK FOR A PLANNED GIFT

These folks believe in your organization. They've supported you for years. Time to ask for a planned gift. They may already have your organization in their will, or might not even have a will. You need to make a clear ask in your direct mail, online, in person at special events and during one-to-one meetings. Be sure to make a planned gift yourself before asking others.

ORGANIZE A PHONE-A-THON

30% of all unrestricted commitments are raised by tele-fundraising. Remember to ask for donors' cell phone numbers. The younger your base of donors, the more likely it is they won't have a landline.

Ask all board members to participate. They don't all have to ask for money. Some will need to bring food, some will record pledges, some will work the phones.

ALWAYS COORDINATE YOUR ASK WITH THE PERSON IN CHARGE OF DEVELOPMENT

Nothing will make a fundraiser angrier than hearing the "great news" that a volunteer got $500 from a prospect when there was a $50,000 ask on the table. It makes everyone look foolish and ultimately will effect your bottom line. Whether you have staff or not, there needs to be a procedure before asking for a gift.

EXAMPLE: A board member casually asked a buddy on the golf course for a major gift. The executive director already had a meeting planned with the potential donor and his new bride, wife number 3. When she heard about the tee-time ask, she went ballistic, cancelled the meeting and insisted that the organization was trying to work around her. It devolved from there, and the nonprofit lost big time.

CHOOSE A LIMITED AMOUNT OF MATERIALS TO BRING BEFORE YOUR ASK

People want different levels of detail. Before making a philanthropic decision, some folks might want to see your financials, talk to clients, meet additional staff or board members, or get a formal proposal.

Do not bring everything you have to the first meeting. It is all about the donor and what he or she wants. It also gives you an opportunity to get in touch again.

ASK YOUR DONOR WHAT HE OR SHE KNOWS ABOUT YOUR ORGANIZATION AND ITS CAUSE

Major donor solicitation is about listening, not talking. One of the first questions should be, "What do you know about our organization and mission?" You might find that this person has a great deal of knowledge, misinformation, regard for or distain for your group. This is a great place to start.

EXAMPLE: A board member on an environmental organization who was a banker went to ask a lady for a gift. He spoke with great passion and at great length about the mission and the need for land reclamation. Had he bothered to ask what she knew about the organization and its mission, he would have discovered that she had a PhD in botany and had written the literature that he was incorrectly referring to. Fortunately, she was both kind and generous, straightened him out and sent him off with a signed copy of her book and a check. He never went on another call without doing his homework, listening more and talking less.

USE YOUR
BOARD RETREAT
TO TRAIN YOUR
BOARD MEMBERS
IN HOW TO
"MAKE THE ASK."

GET FUNDRAISING TRAINING

You might want to bring someone in for a board retreat (a list of facilitators is in the resource section) and train the entire board. You might also want to attend a local meeting of AFP (the Association for Fundraising Professionals www.aftnet.org) or travel to their national meeting or take a course on fundraising at your local college or university, or online.

THE BOARD OF WILLOW'S WAY CHOSE THE HERMANHOF WINERY FOR ITS FUNDRAISING TRAINING RETREAT. IT WAS A GREAT SETTING FOR LEARNING, RELAXING AND TEAMBUILDING. (I'M THE RED-HEADED DUMPLING ON THE FAR LEFT.)

KNOW WHO IS CURRENTLY SUPPORTING YOUR CAUSE

When you go in to ask for money, people want to know who the other donors are. We want to donate where the "smart money" gives. Also, you will want to know their relationship to the prospect. For instance, you might want to be able to say, "Your neighbors Lucy and Stanley have been donors for 5 years, as is your retired partner Mr. XYZ, and we have just gotten a marvelous contribution from the children's program at your church."

Be sure, however, to respect donor privacy. Don't share donor names without prior authorization from the organization's executive director or development officer. He or she can tell you whether or not the donor has permitted the organization to use his or her name for purposes of fundraising. And never state the gift amount without expressed permission from the donor. A quick phone call from the organization's development staff is often all it takes to obtain the necessary permission and will signal to the donor that serious efforts are made to protect privacy.

ASK YOUR CHURCH FOR A "SECOND COLLECTION"

The church passes the plate for its own collection and then you or someone from your organization gives a brief talk (or sometimes the whole sermon) about your group and the plate is passed again; the proceeds go to your group.

From "Fifty-Three Ways for Board Members to Raise $1000" by Kim Klein, reprinted with permission of *The Grassroots Fundraising Journal*, www.grassrootsfundraising.com.

WRITE A LETTER TO YOUR FRIENDS REQUESTING FUNDS

Write a letter on your own stationery. Explain why you believe this to be a good philanthropic investment. Share that you are already a donor and tell how the money is going to be spent. Before you mail those letters, however, make sure you have discussed this with the group's executive director or development director to make sure that your letter fits in with the organization's on-going development strategy.

EXAMPLE: A friend of mine poured out her heart in a brilliant letter disclosing her personal experience as an abused child. She talked about how she weighed 340 lbs. at age 24 and how she had lost 200 pounds and fought to gain back her self-respect. She talked about how her brother had spent more than 50% of his life in prison.

78% of the people who received her letter sent a donation. She was disappointed with the other 28%. We need to support our supporters when they make a bold move and also educate them about direct mail response rate. She was shocked when I told her that a response of 10% would have been phenomenal.

ASK YOUR VOLUNTEERS FOR A DONATION

Far too many organizations believe that because someone gives their time, they shouldn't be asked for money. Exactly the opposite is true. Because someone invests their time, they have the perfect reason to build on their investment and give their money. Why give to another organization that they don't know as well?

The best person to ask a volunteer is another volunteer who has already given.

IF YOU ARE GOING INTO A PUBLICLY-TRADED CORPORATION, GET THE STOCK PRICE FOR THE DAY

You can start the conversation by sharing your knowledge about how the company is doing. If the stock is up, you say, "Well it is a great day at XYZ Corporation. Our stock is up." If it is down, you can say, "Well, it's a great time to make the community a little healthier, as our stock seems to have the flu." Obviously, if you refer to yourself as a stockholder, you have to buy stock before your visit.

HAND ADDRESS ENVELOPES TO TOP DONORS

A lot of mail goes straight from the mail box into the trash without being opened. No passing go, no collecting $200 dollars. One of the exceptions is mail in hand-addressed envelopes. Take the time to address the envelopes. If you know the recipient, include your name on the return address.

EXAMPLE: I live in a condo building. I watch my neighbors at the mail box throw unopened letters into the trash like they are dealing poker. When I do a little peeking, it is always the letters with the handwriting that go upstairs with them.

SELL TICKETS TO EVENTS OR RAFFLES TO BENEFIT YOUR NONPROFIT

My friend Marty told me years ago, "Never sell a ticket, always sell a table." When approaching someone, sell one table, not one ticket.

The question should always start with, "How many tables would you like to buy to support our efforts to…?" Then state your mission.

...A THOUGHTFUL GIFT THAT REFLECTS
YOUR PROSPECT'S INTERESTS

4

STEWARDING...

YOUR DONORS

Businesses call stewardship "relationship management." Mothers call it "minding your manners." It is the art and science of making sure that the people who give to your organization feel appreciated and want to stay involved. For the most part, it is done incredibly poorly, yet it is the easiest way to get board members involved. When I speak to a group of donors and say, "Tell me a story about the last time you felt your gift was really appreciated," they look at me like I asked, "Tell me about your last bungee-jumping experience."

There is an old axiom: "Find 7 ways to thank your donors and they will quickly give again." Are you thanking once? Twice? At all?

Expressing gratitude is a marvelous place in the process for those who hate to ask to get involved. The more personal the thank-you, the higher the chances for a second and larger gift. Always think about creativity, warmth and keeping the costs low.

WRITE A THANK-YOU NOTE FOR A DONOR VISIT

You don't necessarily have to handwrite a thank-you note, since many of us, thanks to constant typing, have sub-par handwriting. E-mail is all right, "snail mail" is much more powerful. Mention specific points that your donor made. For instance, "Since your mother was a friend of Rachel Carson and was concerned about the environment long before it became fashionable, you might want to consider naming this initiative after her." Also, include any requested materials and always end with your plan for the next meeting. "As we discussed, I will call you next Wednesday to set up a meeting with your brother and sister."

CALL DONORS AND THANK THEM FOR THEIR GIFTS

Fundraising guru Penelope Burk has done research on the power of a phone call from a board member. The assumption is that because you aren't paid, your call is from the heart. (We know that staff also care deeply.) You need a script to do this effectively. It is also an opportunity to collect data on your donors such as:

✓ What stage of life are they in? If you don't have great records, how long have they known about your organization and how long have they been donors?

✓ How did they get involved in the first place?

✓ What are their preferences? What appeals resonate best with them?

✓ What could you be doing better?

✓ What do they most appreciate about the work you are doing now?

EXAMPLE: A board member called a donor and was immediately asked by the donor what else she could do. The donor's husband had died of the disease that this organization was committed to cure. The board member set up a meeting with the executive director, and the donor ultimately became a board member, a much larger donor and solicited a free audit from her husband's brother.

THANK YOU!

THANK YOUR SUPPORTERS (WITH THEIR PERMISSION) IN A VERY PUBLIC WAY

The Lakeshore Educational Foundation in Michigan asked donors to fund a message sign for their school. The 100 or so donor names rotated on the screen with the words, "The LEF thanks you for supporting the landscaping project."

GIVE A BOARD MEMBER OR COMMITTEE CHAIR A GIFT WHEN THEY TAKE ON A BIG TASK

You need to have an internal culture of graciousness before you thank your external supporters. Before you raise any dollars, you need to get your team together. Encourage your folks when they say yes to an assignment. You might want to give an event chair a leather folder with an engraved plate that says, "Mary Smith, Gala Chair, 20XX" to use as she plans the event, or "Hector Gonzalez, Chair of Nominating 20XX." Include the notes of prior chairs.

RESOURCE: A great web site for interesting ideas is www.ThingsRemembered.com.

GIVE A DONOR A CARD CASE THAT SHOWS YOU KNOW WHAT HE OR SHE CARES ABOUT

For the donor who has everything, personalize a business card case with a photo. Perhaps for a golfer, Photoshop your donor's face between Tiger Woods and Arnold Palmer. For the cyclist, photo shop your donor in the yellow jersey crossing the finishing line in the Tour de France. Or have a photo of your donor in front of the building she's just financed. The cases are available at www.Artscow.com.

CALL A DONOR AND THANK THEM FOR A GIFT

Even the most ask-averse board member can feel comfortable thanking current donors. Research shows that this vastly improves your retention rate. It's also a great opportunity to find out why someone gave. The trick is to make it a true thank-you and not a pitch for more money.

EXAMPLE: One board member was making thank-you calls and asked the donor why she gave. The donor said, "I had a son with this disease." The key word was "had." This turned into a 55-minute call.

The two women really connected. The donor mentioned the date of her son's death. The board member wrote it down and called the next year the day before the anniversary to tell the donor she was thinking about her. This has been going on for 7 years now. The donor is now a planned giver and although the two women live in different cities and connect only once a year, the board member says that this friendship was the greatest gift of her board service.

ABOVE: BUSY NEUROSURGEON, WIFE AND MOTHER DR. EDIE ZUSMAN MAKES STEWARDSHIP CALLS ON BEHALF OF THE EPILEPSY FOUNDATION.

SEND A PERSONAL THANK-YOU NOTE TO YOUR GUESTS FOR ATTENDING YOUR EVENT

There is nothing like a personal thank-you note thanking someone for attending an event. State why the cause is important to you and what the funds are going to be used for.

EXAMPLE: After a golf tournament for the National Council on Alcoholism and Drug Abuse, I sent a thank-you letter to the 180 participants and explained that I was on the board because my brother-in-law died of alcoholism at 43 and I had promised my mother-in-law before she died that I would work on this issue. I shared the specifics of the work NCADA does and wrote personal notes for the golfers I knew. A number of folks then thanked me for the thank-you note!

Valet Parking

GIVE YOUR MAJOR DONORS PRIORITY OR FREE VALET PARKING

This is appreciated at hospitals, schools, and cultural events. The older the donor and the colder your climate, the more it is appreciated.

EXAMPLE: One very wealthy donor to a hospital said that he gave because the hospital gave him a pass for free parking. This seemed somewhat ludicrous given his income, but when questioned he said, "The other hospital in town wasn't interested in what my thoughts were about how the hospital is run and I hate to pay for parking." The hospital he gives to is now working with him on the possibility of endowing a parking garage.

WRITE A HANDWRITTEN NOTE TO A DONOR FOR A CONTRIBUTION

For those of us with legible writing, a handwritten note on your own stationary is marvelous. Be sure to mention you are a board member. You may want to share with the donor how the money will be spent, or a personal story of why you are involved. Do not ask for more money. The note will shock and delight people!

EXAMPLE: A Red Cross volunteer writes personal thank-you notes and always mentions that his daughter had been in an accident and thanks to the Red Cross had received massive blood transfusions during surgery. He says that his daughter had also learned to swim and to babysit from the Red Cross. He says that although blood services is only one small aspect of the work of the Red Cross, there would be no photo of her son—his grandson—on his desk without generous donors.

THANK A CORPORATE DONOR AT THE POINT OF PURCHASE

If a corporation is a sponsor, the next time you purchase a product, thank the salesperson or server for the donation. Share with them that the company's support influenced your buying decision. They will feel proud of their employer and share the news. You might even recruit a volunteer or new donor or get a new client this way.

EXAMPLE: One board member switched his local latte purveyor and told the owner, "I don't like your coffee as much as your competitor's, but I like your generosity to the community."

SEND A POSTCARD TELLING HOW A DONOR'S MONEY HAS BEEN SPENT

Part of thanking people is letting them know how their money was used. Creating a series of postcards throughout the year with a photo of how your mission is being carried out reminds donors how they have helped. For instance, for Veteran's Day, send a postcard that reads, "Larry XYZ served our country bravely in WWII. Now, thanks to your generous donation, former Corporal XYZ is able to ....."

SEND YOUR DONORS A LOTTERY TICKET

As a thank-you, send a lottery ticket with a note that says, "We know we are 'the new game in town' and appreciate your taking a chance on us," or, "We won the lottery when you committed to prevent child abuse (or whatever) and hope you feel the same way. We will keep you informed of what we've done with your investment in our cause."

Obviously, since this technique involves gambling it has to be used judiciously. As with any gift, "know thy donor" needs to be your mantra.

CREATE A PERSONALIZED VIDEO FOR A DONOR TO THANK THEM FOR A GIFT

Video a recipient of services and thank a donor by name. For instance, e-mail a video of a student sharing the message, "Mr and Mrs. XYZ, thank you for supporting our science fair. This is my project. I developed a method to…" or perhaps an elderly person saying, "Mr. And Mrs. XYZ, this is the new wheelchair ramp for my house your gracious gift paid for. My husband and I have been living here for 52 years and now…"

SEND A BIRTHDAY OR ANNIVERSARY CARD TO YOUR DONORS

You can get their birthdates if they are signed up on a social networking system like MySpace, LinkedIn or Facebook. If everyone else is sending them e-mail, send them a real card. It just takes a few minutes and a stamp.

You remember your donors and they will remember you!

INVITE TO LUNCH A PAST FUNDER WHO IS ON HARD TIMES AND DON'T ASK FOR MONEY

Just as our nonprofits go through hard times, so do our donors. Some recent instances: The burst of dot-com, the downing of an aircraft, the implosion of Enron, the victims of Bernie Madoff, a personal setback such as a divorce, and the list goes on. Donors helped you when you needed them. Be there when they need you. They will not forget you in years to come. And it's the right thing to do.

EXAMPLE: A development director at a small Midwestern college read in the paper about the collapse of the consulting firm Arthur Anderson. She called a major donor who was a partner at Anderson and said, "I read what is going on with your firm. Can I buy you lunch?" The alum said, "As long as you're buying and not asking, I certainly have the time." She not only bought him lunch, but was able to share his resume. With his permission, she also brought another donor who was looking for a CFO. Six weeks later, her donor had a new position and she had a lifelong friend.

What are you doing for your donors when they are faced with difficult situations?

HOLD A THANK-YOU PARTY FOR DONORS

A recognition event can be anything from a morning breakfast to a black-tie dinner at a country club to a backyard barbecue to cookies and milk in a church basement.

It is important to dispel any perception that money that should be going to the mission is being spent on entertaining.

Share with your guests how their money is being used.

EXAMPLE: When my husband and I were stationed at Fort Bragg, North Carolina, we became donors to the Little Theater. They treated us like Bill and Melinda Gates. In addition to wonderful theater, we were invited to a champagne brunch and an opening night party. They made every guest feel like they had made a brilliant move by becoming a part of the theater guild. They also made it clear that the events were sponsored by local theater lovers.

HAVE A "BREAKFAST OF CHAMPIONS" EVENT TO THANK YOUR MAJOR DONORS

Photoshop your donors' photos and put them on Wheaties boxes. Be sure to invite their families. Share with them and their families the impact of their gifts.

Be sure to let the champions take home their boxes.

EXAMPLE: Karyn Buxman created the Wheaties boxes (above) for speakers who donated their time at a National Speaker's Association event. Twenty years later, Shep Hyken still has his Wheaties box in his office.

HAND-DELIVER A MUG TO YOUR SUPPORTERS

Fill your new mugs with candy, coffee or some other treat and hand-deliver to your supporters.

The mug should have your agency name, phone number, web address, logo and, if you have one, a tag line about what you do.

You might also want to give a supply to the front line staff to give to people who make their job easier. Whether it is a nurse, secretary, judge, case worker, principal, parking lot attendant or whoever, it will pay big dividends in terms of achieving your mission.

HONOR LOYAL DONORS AS WELL AS LARGE DONORS

We tend to recognize big givers. Honor loyal donors as prominently. In your printed material, honor both large donors and donors who have given for a long time. If you have a recognition dinner or special event, have a way to make sure you let your longtime supporters know they are appreciated. (If you don't have great records, time to start!) Loyal donors are also more likely to be planned givers.

EXAMPLE: United Ways now has a giving society called "Diamond Donors." These are folks who have given for 25 years or longer. When speaking at a diamond event in Jacksonville, Florida, I met a remarkable man who had been giving for more than 50 years. He said that the precursor to United Way, the Community Chest, had helped his brother when he had polio. His father had told him that it saved his brother's life and that he should always give whatever he could. We asked him to share his story and, with tears in his eyes, he told the crowd his father's words.

CREATE A POSTER FOR YOUR ORGANIZATION

You might want to commission a poster or have a contest to design one. Your posters can be sold to the general public or given framed to your major donors. The posters should include the name of your organization, your web site and the year the poster was printed. When you produce the next year's edition, raise the price of last year's poster.

Donors at certain price points should get a framed, signed copy.

EXAMPLE: In the early 1990's, artist Mary Englebreit donated some of her art work for a series of posters to benefit The Family Resource Center. The posters are still proudly hanging in homes and businesses today.

PUT YOUR DONOR'S PHOTO ON THE WALL IN YOUR OFFICE, WAITING ROOM OR BOARDROOM

When creating a donor photo gallery, honor not only large donors but also donors who have given for many years. You might also want to give your donors the option of having a family photo so that the next generation will be encouraged to make your organization part of their future giving.

Arrange for a photographer to take the photos.

Have a ceremony once a year when the new photos go up. You might want to consider using your annual meeting for the event.

SEND YOUR DONORS LIFE SAVER CANDIES

This is a great thank-you for organizations that work in the relief area or for someone who came to the rescue at the last minute.

EXAMPLE: I was doing a keynote in San Antonio and the next speaker's plane was grounded in another city. The meeting planner was frantic. A major donor who was also a board member volunteered to give a speech. The planner sent her assistant across the street to Woolworths and bought out the Life Saver stash. At the end of a brilliant speech, the board member received a basket of candies. He beamed and said, "This is one of the best presents I've ever received."

WHEN YOU RECEIVE THE GIFT OF TIME, GIVE A WATCH OR CLOCK WITH YOUR LOGO

For your volunteers, whether participating in the board room, giving a free accounting, or legal advice, or helping with I.T. marketing or secretarial work, give a watch or clock with your logo, website and phone number as a thank-you.

GIVE FLASHLIGHTS OR CANDLES TO A MAJOR DONOR WHO LIGHTS THE WAY FOR OTHERS

To say thanks, if it's in your budget, put your logo on a flashlight or have one of your glue gun-slinging board members come up with a creative way to display your info on a candle. It can be anything from a camping lantern to a basket of candles in your donor's favorite color.

EXAMPLE: When I was a board president, there was a board member who was a visionary leader, a generous man and a great strategic thinker. I found a collection of 12 flashlights from a Big Bertha to a keychain-sized one. At the presentation, every guy on the board was green with envy. (There might be something on the Y chromosome to account for this.)

FOR YOUR DONORS OF LONG DURATION, SEND THEM A TAPE MEASURE

Send a note that says, "It is hard to measure how much we value your years of support. Please know that we appreciate you." Put your logo, phone and website on the tape measure.

HAVE A PRIVATE INFORMATIONAL EVENT FOR YOUR LONGTIME DONORS

These folks have been giving for years. This event should be in addition to one-on-one attention. You might want to have a panel of experts discuss ongoing research, the future of the symphony or advances in preschool education. Let your donors ask questions and share their views in small groups.

Don't forget that many people who give are not "gala people" and might prefer information to hors d'oeuvres.

HOLD A "THANK-A THON"

This is a group gathering where you get together and thank current donors. Be sure to have a script, whether personalized or generic. Also, have a mechanism to follow up with folks who need additional information, have specific ideas or want to get more involved as volunteers or board or committee members.

Thank-a-thons can be held at the development offices of universities with phone banks, real estate offices or any other site with a large number of phones.

Ask your volunteers to arrive at least 30 minutes early for training.

Be sure to make it fun. Offer prizes for the first person to reach X number of people and have pizza delivered for the volunteers to enjoy when they need a break.

Remember that everyone doesn't have to staff the phones. There need to be I.T. folks and food volunteers and the ubiquitous clean-up committee.

THANK YOUR STAFF PUBLICLY

Your entire organization should have "an attitude of gratitude." Nonprofits ask a lot of their employees. As with volunteers, board members and donors, recognition should never be overlooked.

ABOVE: LYNNE RAJANI, THE EXECUTIVE DIRECTOR OF REBUILDING TOGETHER, ST. LOUIS, PRESENTING FLOWERS TO HARDWORKING DEVELOPMENT DIRECTOR LAURA HURT AT THEIR ART AUCTION

YOU NEED TO CREATE A BUZZ...

5

Have you ever said, "We are the best-kept secret in town?" Part of the fundraising cycle is educating others about what your organization does, why it deserves funding and why you became involved. Marketing is a major component of fundraising. Creating positive "buzz" will enhance all your fundraising efforts.

EXAMPLE: An older board member railed about putting money in the budget for marketing. He claimed, "Everyone knows us. We've been around forever." The executive director asked him if Coca Cola still marketed even though everyone knew the company. He didn't budge. She then asked him to survey his children's friends about the agency and see what they knew. They were in their late thirties and capable of giving. He was stunned to discover that his kid's friends had never heard of the agency. Marketing stayed in the budget.

WRITE A RESEARCH-BASED OPINION PIECE FOR THE NEWSPAPER

Tell the story of how your organization is addressing an issue in the news.

EXAMPLE: If you are an organization devoted to child abuse prevention, write about how unemployment effects the rate of child abuse. List three things readers can do to prevent abuse as well as information on upcoming events, your web site, and the way you work with families. This article would be appropriate for the local newspaper, mass media, and specialty parenting magazines. Obviously, this should be coordinated with your P.R. department, marketing committee or board members.

LINK YOUR WEB SITE TO YOUR NONPROFIT'S SITE

If you have your own web site, link your site to your nonprofit's and explain why you are involved. You can do this on your board roster and your organization's site as well.

TELL YOUR COWORKERS THAT YOU ARE INVOLVED IN A NONPROFIT

There will be times when you need to solicit money, talent or time or ask colleagues to cover for you at work. Get your coworkers involved from the beginning.

WRITE AN INFORMATIONAL ARTICLE FOR YOUR WEB SITE

Make sure that your organization is recognized as an expert on your cause and easily searchable on the web. Be sure to put the keywords in the title of your article.

CREATE A PIN THAT INVITES INQUIRY

What do you think these pins are all about?*

Halbert Sullivan is a big, tough-looking guy. When asked what his "Don't Shake" button means he responds, "What do YOU think it means?" Mr. Sullivan explains that it means to never shake a baby. He then tells folks about the Father's Support Center, where he helps men become fathers.

Colorectal cancer survivor Edward Leigh, MA, created this pin to humorously illustrate that people who have had part of their colon removed are now called "semicolons." After hearing about the pin's meaning, people always smile. He then discusses the importance of colorectal cancer screening.

TELL THE PRESS ABOUT YOUR AFFILIATION

Send a press release to the local paper, the business newspaper, your company's P.R. department, your church bulletin and your professional association. You get publicity for your nonprofit as well as let people know you are a resource should they need help.

EDIT A FELLOW BOARD MEMBER'S STORY

Some of us are great writers; some of us have other talents. If you are a gifted editor or writer, interview a fellow board member or client and write up their story. Have them proof it to make sure you've accurately captured their thoughts.

This write-up can be used for press releases, online publications, newsletters, etc.

TELL YOUR FRIENDS ABOUT YOUR BOARD MEMBERSHIP

Most of us have limited time. Sharing the news of nonprofit service can offer opportunities to see friends whether at a committee meeting or a fundraising bike ride or walk. Let friends know early on what you are doing and why and how they too can get involved.

TELL YOUR ALUMNI ASSOCIATIONS THAT YOU HAVE JOINED A BOARD

Let former classmates know what you are involved in. They will come to you with their needs, their opinions and ultimately their money, but first they need to know you are involved.

EXAMPLE: One board member wrote her high school alumni magazine that she was on the board of a battered women's shelter. A former classmate called because she "had a friend" who was being beaten. The board member helped her classmate get help. Later, members of the entire class got involved with the cause.

TELL YOUR FAMILY ABOUT YOUR COMMITMENT OF SERVICE

Obviously, your immediate family needs to be involved in your decision to serve, but your extended family needs to know as well. This is a great opportunity to share your values. You may find that someone close to you shares your enthusiasm for the organization's mission and would like to get involved or wants to volunteer for a different reason.

EXAMPLE: A client of mine was a board member who told his sisters that he had joined a board of an organization that was having a walk-a-thon. They got involved because they had just had babies and wanted to train together as well as support "their baby brother." The cause was irrelevant to his sisters. The family support, the shared camaraderie and the opportunity to lose their baby weight made it a successful endeavor.

MAKE SURE YOU HAVE A CLEAR BRAND

Do you have marketing materials that clearly represent your organization and its mission in an integrated fashion? Consistency is everything from the name of your organization to your stationary to your website design to your logo.

If you are a large, well-funded nonprofit, a branding initiative will be the purview of staff, perhaps with the help of an outside consultant. For a smaller nonprofit that is working "lean and mean," it might require more of a collaborative effort between board and staff. Either way, you have to have the tools to tell your story.

WARNING: Be careful about using initials in your branding. MDA may mean Manic Depressive Association, Muscular Dystrophy Association, Montana Department of Agriculture or even The Missile Defense Agency!

SEEK TESTIMONIALS FROM HAPPY CLIENTS

No one sells your mission like happy clients. Without violating HIPAA, other laws or moral codes, ask your former students, audiences, and clients to share how your organization made a difference in their lives. It can take the form of a video interview, an audio archive, a written interview, a photographic history or a creative combination. You will find lots of ways to use these testimonials. Don't forget to secure releases.

Remember, happy clients also become donors. And don't assume that because people aren't wealthy today, they won't become major donors in the future or that they don't know potential major donors.

EXAMPLE: A domestic abuse counseling service asked a former client to come back to speak at its annual meeting. She told of her history of incest at age 10, her struggle with drugs and her disastrous marriage. She shared that she was suicidal when she joined a therapy group three years before. She now had a GED, completed a year of junior college, regained custody of her children and was learning what it was like to pay taxes, the one thing about being "straight, clean and working" that she didn't enjoy. She profusely thanked everyone for letting her tell her story. She said, "This is better than being on Oprah. Unless of course, I got a car. But then, there are those darn taxes again!"

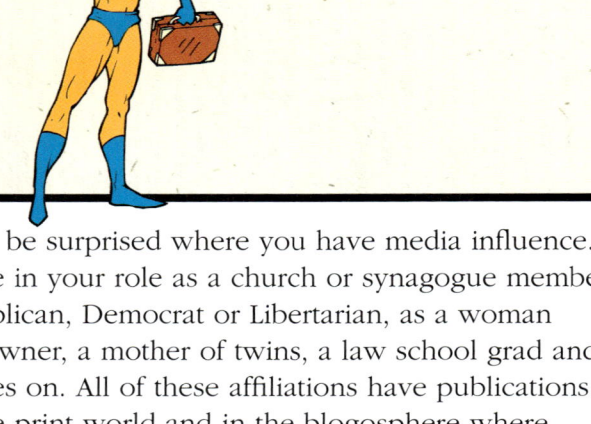

CULTIVATE MEDIA CONTACTS WITHIN YOUR SPHERE OF INFLUENCE

You might be surprised where you have media influence. It might be in your role as a church or synagogue member, as a Republican, Democrat or Libertarian, as a woman business owner, a mother of twins, a law school grad and the list goes on. All of these affiliations have publications both in the print world and in the blogosphere where you can share opportunities to give time, money and information.

IN YOUR FAMILY CHRISTMAS LETTER, BE SURE TO MENTION YOUR BOARD SERVICE

Whether you are sending an e-letter or a "snail mail" greeting, if you send a holiday missive, share the news of your board service.

RECRUIT AN ARTIST OR HAVE A CONTEST TO CREATE TERRIFIC LOGO-WEAR

Great logo-wear turns you and your supporters into walking billboards. The pink ribbon lets folks know that you care about breast cancer. Save the Children Federation has a terrific line of neckties. Remember that not everyone wears t-shirts or carries a canvas bag. What can you put your logo on? You might want to have a high-end gift that represents gifts from major donors.

What can you create and sell to make both money and a splash for your organization?

SELL A PRODUCT AT A SPORTING EVENT

Whether a high school football game or major league baseball game, ask that your organization be allowed to sell a product in the stands or out front to benefit your organization. Make sure you have great signage and ask your volunteers to wear their logo-wear.

If a professional team, ask the players' spouses to get involved. And don't forget to get coverage on the scoreboard.

You will probably make more friends than money. This is usually a marketing rather than a fundraising outing. Keep track of how much you are earning per hour per volunteer.

6

MAKING..

SPECIAL EVENTS

Special events are the lifeblood of many nonprofits. The trick to being successful is to know what success looks like. Is the purpose of your event to cultivate donors, to ask for money, to thank current donors, or to celebrate a milestone or to educate around a specific issue? If you say, "All of the above," you will fail. The clearer you are, the more successful you'll be. The purpose of your event has to be clearly communicated to your guests. If they expect to be thanked and are asked for a donation, don't expect pens and credit cards to fly out of their pockets!

RECRUIT A COMMITTEE FOR YOUR EVENT

If you expect your board to serve as your committee, get more than just a vote. Take the time to get specific buy-in. For instance, if you expect board members to bring or buy a table for a dance, ask them each how many tables they will be responsible for BEFORE you decide to have a vote. You might be surprised. The vote might be to approve YOU doing an event on your own.

EXAMPLE: I was doing fundraising training for an arts board and the subject of the dinner dance came up. I asked, "How many of you plan to bring or buy at least one table?" Less than 5 hands went up. Everyone had creative excuses such as, "I don't dance," "I hate wearing a tux," or "We are always out of town in September. Everyone knows that." I expected to hear, "The dog ate my tickets." I asked them what they liked to do for fun. One guy said, "The truth of the matter is that I like to play 'Texas Hold'em' " (a form of poker). Another board member said, "I would bring 5 tables to that event. The majority of the board concurred, and the initiator of the idea said that he would put together a committee of his buddies. Their first "Texas Hold'em For the Arts" event came into being. The first year it netted 400% more than any of their previous dinner dances.

CREATE FABULOUS FUNDRAISING MATERIALS

You need to have a case statement that includes:

- 💲 Why your charity exists, in other words, your mission
- 💲 How you are going to meet those needs or goals
- 💲 What you still need to be able to further your mission
- 💲 How your potential donor can be a part of your organization

CREATE A SPECTACULAR SIGNATURE EVENT

A signature event is one that is unique to your organization and is repeated year after year or, for some organizations, every other year or every five years.

A note of warning about special events: Always ask staff to keep track of the time they spend and subtract the amount they make from the gross. If you have a staff person spending $10,000 worth of time on an event and you net $20,000, subtract the $10,000 in staff time if earning revenue is your primary special event mission. Be honest about how much the event costs. You might be shocked.

Also, evaluate events from time to time to make sure they have not been overdone and you need to find another way to bring in revenue.

© Epilepsy Foundation of America, Inc.
Reprinted with permission.

OVER 9,000 WALKERS CAME OUT FOR THE
THIRD ANNUAL NATIONAL WALK FOR EPILEPSY.

CAROL WEISMAN -- 130

BRING YOUR KIDS AND THEIR FRIENDS TO AN EVENT

It is important to share with your children what you care about, especially if you are leaving your organization in your will. In years to come, they will become not only donors but also volunteers and board members. Depending on the event, they might already make great volunteers, hanging up coats, passing out water at a race, or registering guests at an auction.

CREATE PERSONALIZED INVITATIONS TO BE SENT FROM YOUR COMMITTEE OR BOARD MEMBERS FOR YOUR EVENT

"Bobbins" by Roseanna Morgan

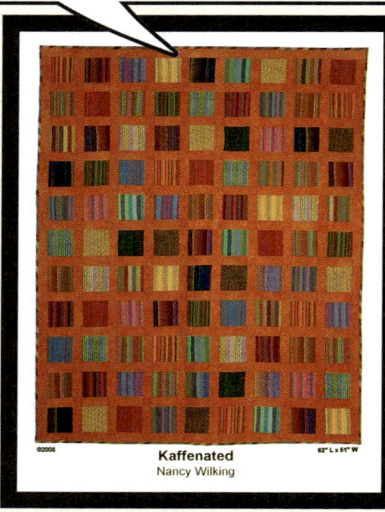

©2008   **Kaffenated**   62" L x 51" W
Nancy Wilking

One of the techniques the Baltimore Heritage Quilters' Guild used to increase attendance to their quilt show from 200 to 1000 was to have individual quilters produce their own invitations. There are many great inexpensive on-line providers for postcards and invitations. I've had great luck with www.kodak.com, www.1800postcards.com and www.modernpostcards.com.

SOLICIT AUCTION ITEMS

If you are a regular at a coffee shop, bagelry or restaurant, ask the business owner/manager/staff to support your organization, as you support their business. This also goes for your bank, broker, hairdresser, and other professionals you deal with. Hopefully, they will also get business.

Look for the win-win. Link your site to theirs, and vice-versa.

Market your event at their venue and be sure to plug their business at your event.

PUT EVENT PHOTOS ON YOUR WEBSITE

People love to see photos of themselves, even if they aren't at their college weight. When you write the captions, spell people's names correctly. When someone Googles their name, their affiliation with you will be apparent.

MAKE EVERY EVENT INTERNATIONAL

All of us have friends across the country, if not around the world. Put your event on the web and send e-mails to all of your friends, relatives, and colleagues.

Have a way for them to participate in your event even if they aren't able to attend, such as buying raffle tickets or making a donation. Make sure you clarify rules regarding pick up or shipping of items, and DO NOT violate local or international gaming laws.

ORGANIZE A UNIQUE TWIST ON AN OLD THEME

Have a sale that is "mission specific." So, if you are an environmental group, have a "green" Christmas sale of items made of recycled goods. If you are an international relief organization, have a sale of "fair trade" goods. You get the picture. You will not only make money, you can recruit volunteers and donors. Be sure to get names, cell-phone numbers and e-mail addresses for future events and donation opportunities.

Don't forget to sell refreshments and set up a membership booth for those who want to join on the spot or seek information or services.

EXAMPLE: Missouri Women in Trades holds a garage sale called "Tool Turnaround." It promotes their mission to help women in the trades. Volunteers solicit friends and employers for tools and use the money they earn for education.

"CHALLENGE A TRADES-WOMAN" IS PART OF THE FUN AT TOOL TURNAROUND

YOUNG SHOPPER BUILDS A TOOLBOX

CREATE A SPEAKER SERIES

You can use a speakers series to cultivate new donors, raise money, get people to your facility or get name recognition. Look for people who are well known in their field. A great P.R. committee is a must. For top speakers, try to get them pro bono, but be prepared to pay big bucks.

EXAMPLE: Maryville University was once a relatively unknown school in St. Louis. Through their speaker series, you hear their name associated with Pulitzer Prize winners, heads of state, Noble Laureates, not to mention folks like Alan Alda and Dave Berry. The Maryville Speakers Series makes money and provides visibility.

CREATE AN "AMBASSADOR TRAINING PROGRAM" FOR YOUR EVENT

Some people at your event will know nothing about your organization. Train some of your board and volunteers to "work the crowd" and introduce themselves to guests to tell more about your organization. They will need to know basic facts. You might want to have your ambassadors come 30 minutes early for training. The goals of an ambassador program are to find out if your guests are potential major donors, board members or clients. Have business cards and be prepared to make a date for a follow-up lunch, dinner or coffee.

You may also want to assign board members responsibility for seeking out and "schmoozing" 3 or 4 specific guests. That way you won't have all the board members concentrating their efforts on a few top donors while other equally important potential donors receive little or no attention. Obviously you need to respect the role of board members who are serving as hosts for their own tables.

The goal is to have your major donor team introduced to as many folks as possible to set up a coffee, lunch or tour as a follow-up to the event.

SAMPLE AMBASSADOR "CRIB SHEET"

SAMPLE GREETINGS:

✓ Hi. I'm _____. I'm so glad you're here. I am board member/volunteer with The Women's Safe House. And you are? (wait for answer)

✓ Welcome to the 30th Birthday Party for The Women's Safe House. Have you been to any of our other events?

✓ Welcome to the 30th Birthday Party for The Women's Safe House. What are you going to do when you turn 30?

NEXT STEPS:

✓ How did you get hooked up with this event?

✓ Have you been involved with The Women's Safe House in the past?

✓ What did you think of the video?

✓ Isn't it amazing that such a serious cause can host such fun events?

...THEN STOP AND LET THEM TALK

THINGS YOU MIGHT WANT TO SHARE ABOUT YOURSELF:

✓ I got involved because:

✓ I am a domestic abuse survivor

✓ My best friend is a survivor

SAMPLE AMBASSADOR "CRIB SHEET" CONT'D

THINGS YOU MIGHT WANT TO SHARE ABOUT YOURSELF CONT'D:

I got involved because:

✓ The Women's Safe House is one of the best-run nonprofits in St. Louis

✓ I have been a volunteer on the hotline for years

✓ I am an attorney and my clients have used their services

WAYS OTHERS CAN GET INVOLVED:

✓ Would you like to take a tour of the shelter?

✓ Would you like to meet our dynamic, mouse-phobic executive director?

✓ Are you a golfer? You have to meet Jennifer Bush, our development director.

✓ Do you like horses? I don't know what the connection is, but you have to meet both Jennifer Bush, our development director, and Dee Dee Simon, our event chair. They both have horses.

✓ Would you be interested in volunteer opportunities? We have a long list of needs for the women in the house. We need financial support for everything from the electric bill to naming opportunities for rooms. I know Jennifer would love to tell you more.

WHAT THE CHARITY HAS DONE:

✓ If you don't know the answer say that you will have Jennifer or Sylvia come over to talk to you or we will send you more information.

✓ In 2008 we sheltered 550 women & children

✓ Nearly 60% of our residents are from the city, almost 30% from the county and the balance from out of state

✓ In current location since 1999

✓ Since then, 5200 women and children have found safety and supportive programs at The House

✓ Since then, have sheltered over 4,000 women & their children

✓ Families may stay up to 12 weeks. Average length of stay 4+ weeks

✓ In 2008 over 525 volunteers

✓ Most women find the Women's Safe House through our Crisis Hotline

OUR FUNDING:

✓ 11% from United Way

✓ Just over 37% from government support

✓ 97% of our client households have incomes of less than $15,000

BOLDLY DISPLAY YOUR "WISH LIST" AT YOUR EVENT*

Much as we all love money, you might need something like a van or a free audit or 50 laptops (not more than 12 months old). Have a large sign with a marker so that your guests can make non-monetary donations.

EXAMPLE: One of my clients that serves battered women mentioned on its wish list at a special event that they needed furniture for their shelter and for women setting up their own households. A man who had just bought a hotel four days before donated 150 rooms of 18-month-old furniture. He was thrilled. He said it was the best event he had ever been to. The shelter thought he was the best guest!

*NOTE: Your wish list should also be in your lobby, on-line and in print publications, bathroom stalls, newsletters, etc. Feel free to ask for anything from an ambulance to 20 hours of data entry to board members with accounting skills or fluency in Mandarin.

TAKE PHOTOS AT YOUR EVENTS AND SEND THE PHOTOS FRAMED TO YOUR DONORS AND SPONSORS

These photos should have your web information and the name of your organization encrypted on the photo. That way, your donors and sponsors have on their walls not only the memory of a good time but also the name of your organization.

DON'T JUST "WHACK AND PLAQUE" RETIRING BOARD MEMBERS-- HAVE AN EVENT TO HONOR THEM

When board members of long and distinguished service retire, have a luncheon or dinner to honor them. Charge a bunch. Speak about what they have done for the organization and how you plan to build on the foundation they've laid.

Introduce them to the current generation of organizational leaders who are carrying on the work that the retired board members started. Let the retirees know that you hope they will want to continue making a difference in the future of the organization through their ongoing contributions.

You will have a mission-focused event that will inspire other board and community leaders.

PARTNER WITH ANOTHER CHARITY ON AN EVENT

This can work particularly well when you don't have donors in common. For instance: a homeless shelter and a choir, a preschool and a geriatric center, a free clinic and a dance company. With this type of pairing you have the opportunity to expand your donor base and share expenses.

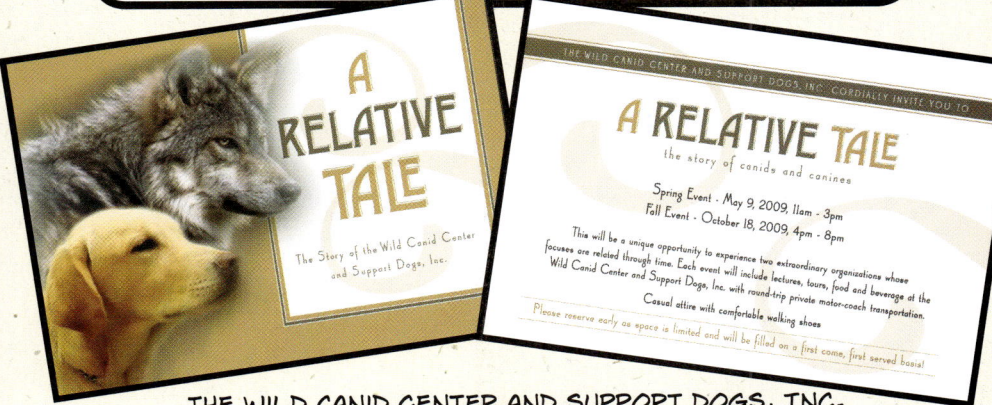

THE WILD CANID CENTER AND SUPPORT DOGS, INC.
PARTNERED ON A FUNDRAISING EVENT TO RAISE FUNDS
AND AWARENESS ON BEHALF OF BOTH ORGANIZATIONS.

GET THE NAMES AND CONTACT INFORMATION OF EVERY GUEST WHO ATTENDS

You want to get the names of every guest who attends so that you can invite them next year and also so that you can thank them for attending this year. If possible, ask them for their e-mail and cell phone* information as well. Don't forget, this is all about permission-based marketing. Ask your guests if they would like information on volunteer opportunities, services or other information. If not, NO SPAM.

*NOTE: The reason you want a cell phone number rather than home or office is that more and more people don't have land lines and if they change jobs or cities, tend to keep their cell phone number.

DON'T HAVE AN EVENT AND INVITE PEOPLE

Have a "non-event" or "phantom event." Invite people to send in money and stay home, put their feet up, rent a movie, read a good book, cook their favorite meal and allow you to spend 100% of their money on doing good.

It's our birthday and in celebration we are having a **Phantom Birthday Party on 15th March 2009.**

We'd like **you** to have a party to celebrate our birthday. Could you celebrate our birthday by hosting a fundraising dinner, lunch or tea at your home, workplace or favourite location?

Rather than send us a present you could send us a donation which will be directed towards ongoing delivery of our trauma services, especially like those we delivered during the recent Victorian bushfires, which further extended our services.

Although our Birthday is 15 March you can host your event anytime in March.

AN INVITATION TO A PHANTOM DINNER CREATED BY DAVID ZERMAN AT THE ROYAL MELBOURNE HOSPITAL, AUSTRALIA.

CREATE AN EVENT THAT RAISES MONEY AND VISIBILITY

Some events earn lots of money, some earn you friends. Consider one that nets you both.

EXAMPLE: In St. Louis, Missouri, Nurses for Newborns Foundation has a yearly gift wrapping program in a local upscale mall. Board members, volunteers and staff are involved.

ASK YOUR GUESTS FOR E-MAIL ADDRESSES AND SEND THEM A THANK-YOU PHOTO FROM YOUR EVENT

Folks enjoy seeing photos of themselves. Sending a thank-you note by e-mail is inexpensive and enters your guest into your system for future e-zines and e-vites.

ASK YOUR CHILDREN TO HAVE A FUNDRAISER WITH THEIR SCHOOL, SCOUT TROOP OR RELIGIOUS SCHOOL

Not only do you bring in dollars, you also educate your children, their friends and parents about your cause. You also train the next generation of donors.

The next year, you might just find your kids coming to you with ideas.

INVITE COMMITTEE MEMBERS FOR AN "M&M" MEETING

In medicine, there are "M&M" meetings, which stands for "Morbidly and Mortality," in other words, a conference on what happened to the patient. In the nonprofit world, we call them "debriefing sessions."

Set ground rules for these sessions. Ask that everyone stay focused on the mission and speak honestly and kindly, recognizing that people have put a great deal of work into an event, or maybe they haven't and feel guilty.

Ask your committee members for their opinion on what worked well and what could be improved on. Consider having inexpensive thank-you gifts. Always have great food.

Discussion issues:

1. Did we meet our goals?

2. Should we do the event again?

3. What did each of the committee members like most?

4. What did members like least?

5. Who is following up with whom? (potential donor lunches and tours, thank-yous to participants, donors, etc.)

IN ADDITION TO A THANK-YOU NOTE TO A MAJOR SPONSOR, PICK UP THE PHONE

A quick thank-you call, even if you just leave a message, really stands out in an e-mail, text-message world. It should include:

1. Something personal, such as "It was marvelous to meet your lovely wife, Nancy."

2. Something about the future: "We look forward to being able to complete the building project thanks to your support."

3. Something about their business: "I hope you had a chance to meet Mr. XYZ. I told him that you would be a great firm to work with."

HAVE A LEGACY PARTY AND DON'T CHARGE ANYONE

Consider a party for your organization where the only ticket for admission is a note from your guest's attorney that your charity is in their will. It might be a small crowd at first, but year after year you will see growth. Of course, it has to be a GREAT party and you will need underwriting, but it will pay big dividends in the long run.

7

GOING..

HIGH TECH

The day this book goes to press, it will be out-of-date when it comes to the creative use of technology in helping fund your cause. The use of cell phones, the web and other electronic devices is exploding.

EVERY nonprofit that needs funds needs at least a web site that has a way to receive gifts.

People give online. If there are any doubts, the Obama campaign should put them to rest.

WRITE AN E-BOOK THAT CAN BE SOLD

An e-book is a downloadable book that can be very short or very long.* For instance, if you serve people with developmental disabilities, write a book on "Employment Issues in Developmental Disabilities." Give 10 free tips on your website, then for more in-depth information, sell the book. The sale of the book might include a monthly update about your cause.

Both the book and monthly update should include a way to become a more active donor.

You also have the chance to segment your list so that you can market more specific opportunities to give. For instance, if you offer information about Hepatitis B, you might have one book for infants and children with Hepatitis B and another book for adults with Hepatitis B.

RESOURCE: Tom Antion's book "Click" available at www.tomantion.com will give you step-by-step details.

CHECK OUT YOUR OWN WEBSITE

Do you have the following components that are recommended by e-fundraising guru Allan Pressel, CEO and Founder of Charityfinders?

- ✓ E-mail List Signup
- ✓ Volunteer Opportunities
- ✓ Employment
- ✓ E-newsletter
- ✓ E-advocacy
- ✓ Petitions
- ✓ E-Cards
- ✓ Forms
- ✓ Public Opinion Poll
- ✓ Questionnaire
- ✓ Referrals
- ✓ User Feedbacks
- ✓ Web 2.0 Tools
- ✓ Discussion/Message Board
- ✓ Chat Room
- ✓ LISTSERV
- ✓ Podcast
- ✓ Blog

PUBLISH A MAGAZINE ABOUT YOUR CHARITY

At MagCloud.com you can print a limited-run magazine about your organization. You can use it to describe your case statement or as a thank-you to major donors. The uses are bound only by your imagination!

When you speak to the folks at MagCloud, mention that you are a nonprofit. They have special rates for us.

PUBLISH A BOOK ABOUT YOUR ORGANIZATION

Through websites like www.mypublisher.com, you can create a four-color hardcover book for as little as $30/book. You can print a book that is the story of your past, a vision of your future or a special event. You can even print a single copy for a specific donor. This book can be used in cultivation, during an ask or as a thank-you.

SHARE YOUR STORY ON YOUR ORGANIZATION'S WEB SITE

People give to people. Sharing your experience with the mission and telling your story well is a powerful fundraising tool. You can share your story in writing, as a podcast, or as streaming video. The technology is endless and the price tag low.

Describe what it felt like to make a contribution and what benefits (psychological, social, and/or financial) you and your family receive from giving.

CREATE YOUR OWN VIDEO AND POST IT ON YOUTUBE

Your organizational video can include anything from an interview with a happy client to a snippet of a performance to remarks from a researcher. You might want to film each of your board members and post why they support your organization.

This video can also be linked to your board members' site or social networking posts such as MySpace and FaceBook.

CREATE A BLOG* ABOUT YOUR CAUSE

Write about your passion. If you are watching your mother struggle with Alzheimer's and you have her permission, write about it. If you are on a mission trip with your organization, share your experience. Others might also be dealing with the early stages of grieving a child's death. This blog must be coordinated with staff and respect confidentiality of all involved.

*NOTE: A blog is an online journal. We used to lock up our diaries and hide them from our siblings. Now we share them with the world. Times have changed!

PURCHASE A SOPHISTICATED DONOR RESEARCH TOOL FOR YOUR ORGANIZATION

If you have a development staff, ask them if they have the tools they need for major donor work. If not, consider making a donation of the services they need so that both you and they can be more productive.

SET UP A GOOGLE ALERT FOR YOUR MAJOR DONORS

This is incredibly simple. You go to www.google.com alerts and follow the instructions. You will receive an e-mail when donors' names appear anywhere on the web. Then write a note or make a call to acknowledge events. It might be the opening of a new office, the marriage of a child or the death of a parent.

You will also want to type in the name of your organization as well as your own name to find out when you are mentioned.

If you try this, you will appreciate having a unique name like Cassandra Smyrniotis rather than a common one like John Smith.

USE SEARCH ENGINE OPTIMIZATION (SEO) TO LET YOUR DONORS KNOW ABOUT YOUR SITE

SEO is the science and art of getting your name to pop to the top of the list when you search for a specific topic. You can purchase words through Google and your name will pop up on the right of the search, depending on what you pay. You can also use words in specific places to get higher rankings.

If you are a nonprofit day care center in Detroit, you might want to purchase "Detroit day care," as well as 10 other combinations of words people might Google. Or, if you want to reach out to donors and clients, and you are a hospice, you might want the links for "hospice San Francisco."

You can Google "fundraising" and thanks to SEO this book will appear to the right.

MAKE IT EASY TO GIVE A MEMORIAL OR CELEBRATORY DONATION ONLINE

You need to be able to make giving easy. It should take under 5 minutes to make a donation online. In addition to making a donation, your donor needs to be able to sign up for more information or to opt out. A "snail mail" as well as an e-mail notification should be sent to both the donor and recipient using an auto-responder.

WHEN FRIEND AND CLIENT DENISE HARRIS NUEHRING HAD TO PUT DOWN HER BELOVED DOG EMILY, I WAS WORKING IN AUSTRALIA. IN ABOUT 3 MINUTES, I WAS ABLE TO SEND A DONATION TO THE HUMANE SOCIETY NEAR DENISE. BY THE TIME I RETURNED HOME, I HAD A RECEIPT AND A LOVELY NOTE FROM DENISE.

LINK YOUR MAILING LIST TO YOUR ORGANIZATION'S VIDEO

You might have a video with high educational content, about the case for giving to your organization, or from media exposure. Make sure that you get this information out to everyone who might be interested.

You can use your own e-mail list or one of your social networking sites such a LinkedIn, Facebook or MySpace to share information about your organization.

EXAMPLE: A charity that provided relief work had a young volunteer working abroad who created a video. She sent this to a friend in the States who did some editing, added music and a poignant 3-minute video was created within 12 hours of the disaster. Two hours later it was posted and sent out, and money was coming in.

WHEN GIVING A TOUR, DON'T BE AFRAID TO SHOW VISITORS WHAT YOU HAVE BEHIND THE CURTAIN...TRUST THAT THEY ALREADY HAVE A HEART, A BRAIN, AND COURAGE.

8

TOURING..

FOR DOLLARS

Many nonprofits give tours. But we make the same mistake: We give the same tour to a prospective patient, student, or client as we do to a prospective donor. A great tour should be personalized. Donors want to know how they can be a part of making the organization better. A prospective client, student or patient wants to know that your nonprofit is already fabulous.

EXAMPLE: I was teaching the director of development of a children's hospital and her staff how to give a tour to perspective donors. I asked her about a room I saw off to the side. She said, "I hate to show people this room. It is one of the children's playrooms. It is dingy and awful." I said, "Guess where you should start your tour?" I was almost blinded by the light that went off over her head.

INTERVIEW YOUR VISITORS BEFORE THEY TAKE A TOUR

People have limited time when touring a facility. An information phone call in advance will help you decide who should be your tour guide, where you should take them, what information they might want and who you should have on stand-by to answer additional questions.

EXAMPLE: An older childless couple was going to visit a hospital for a tour. The natural inclination of the development professional was to pitch a donation to cardiac care, pulmonology or oncology. A brief call giving a number of tour choices revealed that the couple was very close to a niece whose child had been in the neonatal unit for 3 months and had done well. The development director asked the director of neonatology to be available, if possible. She admits that she would have never ever taken this couple near this part of the hospital. Much to the delight of everyone, the ultimate 6-figure gift went to the neonatal unit.

INVITE A LEGISLATOR TO TOUR YOUR CHARITY

The more a legislator knows about your mission, the greater the chance he or she can champion your cause. Make sure to tell your legislator that the press will be there. If there is an earthquake or scandal hogging the news that day, take photos yourself, post them on your website and send them to the media and the legislator's P.R. team.

GIVE YOUR VISITOR A POIGNANT SOUVENIR

What small gift says it all about your organization? A neonatologist in Orlando gives every visitor a preemie diaper with the name of the hospital stamped on it. A therapeutic preschool gives a child's drawing of a house on fire. The assignment was, "Draw a typical evening in your home."

MAKE YOUR TOUR EXPERIENTIAL

Some people learn by seeing, some by hearing and some by touching. Engage all three senses on your tour. If you are a school for learning disabled kids, ask your guests to write one paragraph with their non-dominant hand and with a patch covering their dominant eye. If you are a hospital, teach them to read an x-ray. Get your most creative staff and board members to work on this.

CHARGE FOR YOUR TOUR

You might have a great opportunity to give a seasonal or regular tour. It could involve a rafting trip, actors in a grave yard, historic figures in a church, a symphony or ballet rehearsal, a nature walk with a botanist, or high tea in a historic mansion with the ghost of a long-dead owner.

The tour can be marketed for special occasions, corporate or seasonal events. It can be a perk for donors at a specific level.

ASK YOUR VISITORS IF THEY HAVE FRIENDS WHO THEY WOULD LIKE TO INVITE ON A FUTURE TOUR

A great tour will inspire your visitors to share your story with others. Before they leave or in a follow-up call, ask if they have friends who they would like you to contact to invite. Ask your original guest if there is a group they belong to that should be invited.

BETA TEST YOUR TOUR

Bring in close friends, relatives and new board members to "test drive" your tour. You will want to know:

✓ Was there enough time to ask questions?

✓ Did the guests understand what the organization's needs are?

✓ Were they touched by what they saw?

✓ Did they get bored at any point? If so, where?

✓ How were the amenities (food, bathrooms, etc.)

EXAMPLE: A shelter for battered women gave a test tour to a friend of a board member. When the visitor debriefed, she said that she had planned to donate her business suits until she saw the basement where they would be stored. The basement was quickly removed from the tour and the suit closet mentioned rather than viewed.

9

FINDING..

ADDITIONAL HELP

One of the great joys of working in the nonprofit field is the collegial nature of the work. Unlike some other industries, we tend to be quite chummy. Also, there is a great deal of free or low-cost information to share.

I've included the names and contact information of my pals whom I love to listen to and go to for help. I've also included some of the great books and web sites available.

GREAT FUNDRAISING SPEAKERS & CONSULTANTS

Naturally, if you need a speaker on fundraising, I hope you will call me at 314-863-4422 or e-mail at carol@BoardBuilders.com. However, I am sometimes booked and if I've spoken to your group recently another speaker might make more sense. The good news is that I have some fabulous colleagues. Here are some of my favorites:

CHUCK LORING, MBA, CFRE, www.lascounsel.com, Loring, Sternberg & Associates, phone 954-728-8926; cell 954-328-7086

DAVID ZERMAN and **SARAH BARZEL**, (Australia/Asia) davidzerman@gmail.com; sarah.barzel@gmail.com, International + 61 418 346 999

ALLAN PRESSEL, CEO, www.charityfinders,com, 310-793-793-9707, Powering ePhilanthropy

KIM KLEIN, author of *Fundraising for Social Change,* www.kleinandroth.com; 510-893-8933, ext 306

MARSHALL HOWARD, author of *Let's Have Lunch Together,* www.marshallhoward.com; Marshall Howard & Associates, Toll-Free 877-320-9202

MARGARET MAY DAMEN, CFP®, CLU, ChFC, CDFA, empowers women to create their public and private wealth legacy unique to their passion and purpose to make a difference in the world. 772-223-9015

GAIL PERRY, CFRE, Gail Perry Associates Fired Up Fundraising, www.gailperry.com; Phone 919-821-3050, cell 919-280-0336

JIMMIE R. ALFORD, Founder & Chair, The Alford Group, "Strengthening Not-for-Profits;" www.alford.com; 847-425-9800

FUNDRAISING BOOKS

Let's Have Lunch Together, Marshall Howard

Fearless Fundraising for Nonprofit Boards, Dave Sternberg

Fundraising for Social Change, Kim Klein

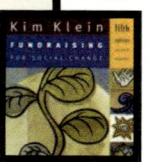

Fired-Up Fundraising: Turn Board Passion into Action, Gail Perry

Beyond The Ask Event: Fully Integrating the Benevon Model, Terry Axelrod

Donor Centered Fundraising: How to Hold on to Your Donors and Raise Much More Money, U.S. Edition, Penelope Burk

Nonprofit Internet Strategies: Best Practices for Marketing, Communications, and Fundraising, Ted Hart, James M. Greenfield, Michael Johnston

People to People Fundraising: Social Networking and Web 2.0 for Charities, Ted Hart, James M. Greenfield, Sheeraz D. Haji

Giving USA 2008: The Annual Report on Philanthropy for the Year 2007, Giving USA Foundation

Raising Charitable Children, Carol Weisman

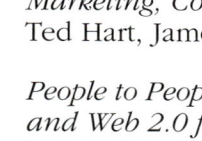

GREAT GOVERNANCE SPEAKERS & CONSULTANTS

If you need a speaker or retreat focused on recruiting dynamic board members, roles and responsibilities of the board, team building and naturally, fundraising, you know my number. Here are some of my super-duper colleagues.

THOMAS BAKEWELL, JD, MBA, CPA, MPH. The guy to call when it is not "business as usual." Great in a crisis when you need a great strategy. 314-965-5511, ThomasBakewell@hotmail.com

STEVEN BOWMAN, www.conscious-governance. com, ConsciousGovernance Global Consultant Australian based, 61 3 9509 9529 steven@conscious-governance.com. Nonprofit strategy, risk, governance and leadership with strategic awareness.

PETER BRINCKERHOFF, Corporate Alternatives, Union Hall, VA. Author of McAdam Award-Winning books: "Mission-Based Management", "Financial Empowerment", "Generations; The Challenge of a Lifetime for Your Nonprofit", and 5 other books. 217-341-3836, peter@missionbased.com, www.missionbased.com

TERRIE TEMKIN, Ph.D., Founding Principal, CoreStrategies for Nonprofits, Inc., CoreStrategies4Nonprofits.com. 888-458-4351 Ext. 83.

HELPFUL WEB SITES

www.AFPNet.org The Association of Fundraising Professionals. Great site for everything from job postings and webinars to local to international meetings.

www.BoardSource.org BoardSource is a resource on board effectiveness and great governance.

www.Grassrootsfundraising.org Lots of good info for groups of all sizes and it's free.

www.Guidestar.org This contains, among other information, the income tax form 990 of U.S. nonprofits.

www.nonprofitrisk.org Nonprofit Risk Management Center. Great way to stay out of jail! Provides risk management assistance and resources for community-serving nonprofit organizations. Many articles and tutorials.

www.CharityVillage.ca Canada's supersite for all things non-profit. Written in English and French.

www.Foundationcenter.org All things grant related.

www.TechSsoup.org Great site for both tech-savvy and novice in the nonprofit world.

www.fundingalert.org The site for *Funding Alert*, a monthly electronic newsletter featuring current grant opportunities organized by funding area.

www.profitcourses.org The site for The Learning Institute for Nonprofit Organizations offers a series of distance education programs with available CEU credit and Certificate of Excellence in Nonprofit Leadership and Management.

GREAT PUBLICATIONS

CHRONICLE OF PHILANTHROPY: The Newspaper of the Nonprofit World offers news for nonprofit organizations on grant seeking, foundations, fundraising, managing nonprofit groups, technology, and nonprofit jobs

NONPROFIT WORLD MAGAZINE: Nonprofit World is a bi-monthly magazine—published since 1983—that provides busy nonprofit leaders with concise and practical articles whose advice can be easily implemented

THE NONPROFIT TIMES: The leading publication for nonprofit management

HARVARD BUSINESS REVIEW: Stimulating information from the for-profit and nonprofit sector. I particularly like the case studies.

ACKNOWLEDGEMENTS

When I sent a note to my buds about proofing this book, there was a resounding "sure." Special thanks to **JOYCE WILBUR** and **ED JOHN** from the United Way of America; **MARGARET MAY DAMEN**, the queen of women and giving; **KIM KLEIN**, who is a world renowned expert on grassroots fundraising; **CHUCK LORING**, who is one of the most talented trainers I've ever heard; **GAIL PERRY**, who wrote one of my alltime favorite books "Fired-Up Fundraising" and who is cute as a button; **MARVA STANHOPE** from the Arthritis Foundation who has the world's greatest shoe collection.

I also want to thank the amazing development professionals I've had the privilege to work with through the years: **MARY ANN LUDWIG**, with the National Hemophilia Foundation, who is a dear friend of many years; and **MARY COLACURCI**, who is not only a joy to work with, but always takes me shopping when I come to Nebraska to work with the Nebraska Children and Family Families Foundation. There are so many others. You know who you are.

I must admit, I have a weakness for Davids. Thanks to **DAVID HULTS**, my favorite career coach; **DAVID LAUBER**, my eye candy; **DAVID SAPHIEN**, my brilliant

ACKNOWLEDGEMENTS

statistician buddy; **DAVID STROM**, writer and techie extraordinaire and the other member of our exclusive book club; and my David half way around the world, **DAVID ZERMAN** and his wonderful wife, **SARAH BARZEL**, who are the world's best host and hostess. What would I do without you in my life?

Thanks to my Chafing Dish pal **ROSE JONAS**, who joins me at the pool 3X/week for hydro and psycho-therapy. And my buddy **TOM BAKEWELL**, who always gives sound business advice and listens to me whine. I so appreciate your friendship. You too, **DICK GOLDBAUM**, my friend and co-author of "Losing Your Executive Director Without Losing Your Way."

I want to thank my mentors (both significantly younger than I!) **PETER BRINCKERHOFF**, who is the only person to win the McAdam Award for the best nonprofit management book, not once, but twice; **ELAINE FLOYD** who knows everything you could ever want to know about publishing; and my friend and speaking mentor **KARYN BUXMAN**, who abandoned Hannibal, Missouri to live happily-ever-after in La Jolla, California with her romantic sweetie **GREG GODEK**.

...CONTINUED NEXT PAGE

ACKNOWLEDGEMENTS

I continue to work with the great executive directors in this world **ANN MACK, ED TASCH, HELEN WRONSKI,** and **BETH DESSEM.** You rock.

I have also had the privilege to mentor emerging leaders in the field. Two who have become family are **DENISE HARRIS NUEHRING** and **ERIN FARRELL.** It is fun to watch you surpass me.

And finally my family. My son **JONO ROBBINS,** who loves his work as a ceramics teacher and who has the world's greatest laugh, and my son **FRANK ROBBINS** who is in grad school in engineering management. I so appreciate your encouragement and support. And **LAURA,** who is a spectacular daughter-in-law. I was awed by your talent as a director off-Broadway in New York and now in St. Louis and most of all, as the mother of our beloved grandson, **FREDDY.**

And **FRANK,** my husband of 33+ years, who schleps books and proofreads and stays at home and waits or comes along to parts unknown, I wouldn't be doing any of this without you. The high point of my day is still when you walk in the door.

PUBLISHING SUPERHEROES

This book would not have been birthed without a band of merry, cranky and quirky superheroes. Meet the team:

NAME	SUPERPOWER
Frank Robbins *Aka Bookman*	Publishing
Elaine Floyd *Aka Processwoman*	Producing Books
Dennis Fletcher *Aka Toonman*	Cartooning
Suzy Gorman *Aka The Shooter* www.suzygorman.com	Photography
Cheryl Jarvis *AKA The Wordmaster*	Editing

ABOUT THE AUTHOR

SUPERPOWERS: Networking, empowering nonprofit leaders, needlepointing , facilitating board retreats, speaking and training on philanthropy, governance and fundraising and getting free upgrades at hotels and on airplanes.

KRYPTONITE: Writing reports, managing detail work and flying coach.

LIFE GOALS: Keeping diabetes under control, keeping husband happy, kids connected and grandson pampered. Would also like world peace and a cure for cellulite.

MOST POPULAR GIGS: Keynotes, retreats and training:
- Getting your entire board involved in fundraising
- Recruiting your nonprofit dream team
- Raising charitable children
- No-snooze meeting
- Roles, responsibilities and joyful board service
- Motivating and rewarding the best of the best

GOALS FOR THIS BOOK:
- Help anxious board members find their superpowers
- Sell 29,010 copies and pay off my mortgage
- Give away enough free e-books (downloadable at www.fundraisingsuperheroes.com) to be in the top 5 listings when you Google "fundraising"
- Get invited to work with your group

ABOUT THE AUTHOR

CAROL AT A BOOK SIGNING FOR RAISING CHARITABLE CHILDREN

CAROL GIVING THE OPENING KEYNOTE FOR THE EPILEPSY FOUNDATION. (SHE IS THE SPECK OF RED WHICH MATCHES THEIR LOGO!)

CAROL AS THE SPOKESBEAR FOR THE BUILD-A-BEAR WORKSHOP HUGGABLE HERO AWARDS

CAROL FACILITATING A RETREAT WITH STUDENT LEADERS AT WASHINGTON UNIVERSITY IN ST. LOUIS. (SHE IS THE OLD ONE IN THE MIDDLE)

WHAT ARE YOU GOING TO IMPLEMENT IN THE NEXT 4 WEEKS?

1. _____
_____

2. _____
_____

3. _____
_____

4. _____
_____

WHAT ARE YOUR SUPERPOWERS?

_____
_____
_____